"Employee handbooks may be th⟨ ⟩ of literature. Every organization has them, but nobody reads them and nobody cares. Now, Robert McFarland has a solution that I can get behind. His new book, *Dear Employee: What Your Boss Wishes You Knew*, is the book every working person needs to read. Sure, we need to know about vacation days, termination policies, and organizational structure, but now, we have a book that covers the really important information that makes an organization work. This is insight that will motivate and inspire you. My only regret is that I didn't have this book at my first job."

Phil Cooke, Ph.D. Filmmaker, media consultant, and author, *One Big Thing: Discovering What You Were Born to Do*

"Whether in personal relationships or the work environment, there are certain universal skills that apply to life: self-examination and communication. It's one thing to know these skills, but another thing entirely to POSITIVELY do them. In *Dear Boss* and *Dear Employee*, Robert provides practical steps to implement these skills in our lives. Robert's work here is refreshing—an excellent reminder that the key to a successful relationship starts with me."

The Honorable Tony Wilt President, Superior Concrete, Inc. Member, Virginia House of Delegates

"Mr. McFarland has again defined the integral elements needed to facilitate meaningful communications and has poignantly articulated them in his new book, *Dear Employee: What Your Boss Wishes You Knew*. His principles have served as a guide for our school to institute transformational reform in how we communicate with each other."

M. E. Black CAPT USN (Retired) Superintendent, Fishburne Military School

"Do bosses have feelings about their decisions and people that they report to—and that report to them? You bet they do! Rock solid research enables the reader to trust the conclusions Robert McFarland digs out in *Dear Employee: What Your Boss Wishes You Knew.* The qualitative and quantitative benchmarks bring the idea that disconnection in the workplace is a reality. McFarland's work emphasizes the human factor as it relates to the bottom line in business. The nuggets that he pulls out of the research and how he relates with everyday life are refreshing. This book will shift your paradigm about bringing your heart to the workplace."

Bob Hasson Co-Author, *The Business of Honor*
CEO, Hasson Inc.
Management and Leadership Consultant

"Want to increase your success and compensation in your work place? Then read Robert's book. It truly is a rare book. We have way too many books on leadership but few books, if any, address how an 'employee' can be a better 'employee.' However, we are all employees in the sense that we all are employed by an organization and report to someone— sole proprietors and some partners being the exception. As the famous philosopher Bob Dylan so eloquently said, 'Everybody has to serve somebody.' Even the President or CEO reports to the board of Directors. The central theme of this book applies to all in the work place: how to use submission as a path to success. Anyone, even the boss, who will practice these principles will not only guarantee themselves promotion after promotion, but new success at home and in your personal life. This book has the potential to change your workplace into a place that engenders this response from the labor force: 'I can't wait to go to work today.' Wouldn't you like to wake up with that attitude each day? If you practice the principles explained in this book, your view of work and your workplace will change drastically, and you will see your paycheck increase as you move up the ladder of success."

Mike Smith President, Home School Legal Defense Association

"A helpful tandem to his first book, *Dear Boss: What Your Employees Wish You Knew*, Robert McFarland's new book, *Dear Employee: What Your Boss Wishes You Knew*, flips the script and helps us all understand what's required to be a model employee by drawing on the best research, grounded in the best source—the Bible. Combining deep wisdom with practical insights, every reader will benefit from this book."

Dr. Jerry A. Johnson President & CEO, National Religious Broadcasters

"Are you easy or difficult to manage? Before you answer that question, you need to read *Dear Employee*. Robert McFarland provides compelling research showing that while your boss's leadership is important, in the end it's your own Self-Leadership that determines your satisfaction on the job. This book is an excellent tool for any organization's leadership development program, and it is must reading for young adults just entering the workforce."

Bill Hendricks Author, *The Person Called YOU*
President, The Giftedness Center
Executive Director, Christian Leadership,
Hendricks Center, Dallas Theological Seminary

"While the title implies this book is for the workplace, it is for anyone who desires to live a life of integrity that encourages others and leverages God-given gifts. That said, I have found that learning to manage your boss is one of the most important, and most frequently neglected, career-building skills. McFarland defines it as Self-Leadership and offers biblically-based pragmatic reflections for cultivating HOPE. Had I read this book earlier, it would have saved me professional angst and the need to ask forgiveness from my former boss! Anyone who complains about their boss (or spouse) can expect a copy of this book from me."

Judith R. Trumbo President/CEO, VMRC

"Self-Leadership or self-governance is the wellspring to integrity, respect, and honor in the workplace. It steers supervisors from the ditch of micro-management and protects employees from the blowout of entitlement mentality. Robert McFarland's practical guidelines keep us in our lane and gets us all back to making a living doing what we love."

Dr. Joseph Umidi Executive Vice President, Regent University
Founder, Lifeforming Leadership Coaching

"Finally a book that exposes the unspoken expectations of the person that holds many of the keys to your success in the workplace—your boss! Read it—apply it—succeed!"

Dr. Randy Carlson CEO, Family Life Communications and Intentional Living

"Once again, my friend Robert McFarland provides another great resource for the workplace. This time, for employees wanting to show good character and leadership in the workplace. I highly recommend this book!"

Tim Wildmon President, American Family Association

"As a young leader in the Navy I was taught to build my success by being a great follower and helping those around me succeed. That included my managers, even if they were not my favorite people. Robert lays out exactly how to do that well in a way that will supercharge your career, joy and passion. Thank you for bringing this perspective to a whole new generation of world-changing leaders!"

John Ramstead CEO, Beyond Influence, Inc.
Host, *Eternal Leadership* podcast

"I learned the hard way that you will never lead others if you can't lead yourself. McFarland's advice on Self-Leadership is worth the price of admission. It is what I wished someone had told me when I was graduating from college."

Hugh Whelchel Executive Director, Institute of Faith, Work & Economics
Author, *How Then Should We Work: Rediscovering the Biblical Meaning of Work*

"As a CEO and researcher, I found myself absorbed in the survey and research findings in *Dear Employee: What Your Boss Wishes You Knew*. The Biblical references are refreshing, and Robert McFarland did an excellent job of nailing down the demeanor and thoughts of today's workforce."

Dr. Arnie Cole CEO, Back to the Bible

"I am thrilled to find a book—although designed for employees (and bosses!)—that is so relationship oriented that I can recommend it to everyone from sports teams to married couples. Thoroughly researched and supported by quotes from well-known authors and business leaders, it's steeped in the authority and credibility decision-makers can depend on."

W. H. Stevens Jr. international award winning film and TV producer, Christian broadcasting executive, and world record powerlifter

"Don't get confused: Robert McFarland's book, *Dear Employee: What Your Boss Wishes You Knew*, is not just for employees but for everyone. It could have been entitled, *Dear One: What Your Maker Wishes You Knew—A Guide to a Fulfilled Life*. Robert presents principles that, if practiced, will enable one to not only be a better employee but develop a fulfilled life of meaning and purpose."

Dick Blackwell, PE Principal, Blackwell Engineering

"Robert McFarland does it again. This time he flips the research so you learn the other side of the story. In *Dear Employee: What Your Boss Wishes You Knew,* you'll discover what's going in the mind of your boss. McFarland offers the data that supports how insufficient acknowledgement, imperfect communication, inadequate work ethic, and a lack of the big picture create unproductive tension. But he doesn't stop there! The rest of the book empowers you to be the bridge that closes the gap. You'll learn how to become an honoring, open, perceptive, and engaged employee. This is your chance to transform the relationship with your boss and create a highly satisfying work experience."

Tami Heim President and CEO, Christian Leadership Alliance

"The gulf between a boss and an employee can be a wide one. Robert's work to bridge that gap—through this book and his *Dear Boss*—is important and provides the type of practical advice needed to convert theory to reality. Thank you, Robert, for this fine work!"

Mark Hancock Chief Executive Officer, Trail Life USA

"Using research as the starting point and Scriptural principles as the road map, Robert McFarland explores what bosses wish their employees knew in order to create a healthy and thriving workplace. McFarland's principle of 'self-leadership always preceding team leadership' is ground-breaking. I only wish I had been taught these insights early on in my calling as a pastor."

Dr. John F. Sloop retired pastor

"*Dear Employee: What Your Boss Wishes You Knew* should be given out alongside the employee handbook in companies everywhere. Staff who take to heart the author's insights on team participation, accountability, integrity, discipline—and so much more—will themselves become leaders. Robert McFarland (no relation, as far as I know) is a trusted voice in leadership and organizational theory. We eagerly look forward to everything he publishes."

Dr. Alex McFarland author, educator, entrepreneur

"Robert's books have touched on some key areas critical to success in our organizations. I appreciate his willingness to use faith as a guiding principle in how we look at these workplace relationships. His mix of stories and real data brings credibility to his message. This book as well as his first can serve as a wonderful guide to building a healthy and productive team."

Wayne Witmer President, Harman Construction, Inc.

"Finally a book that shows you how you can take charge of yourself and your future. Stop complaining about your life or your job or your boss, and do something about it. Read *Dear Employee* and do what Robert McFarland says. You'll be glad you did."

Star Parker, Founder and President, Center for Urban Renewal and Education

"Great leaders across this country are burning out. A wild fire is blazing at the employee level that is destroying organizations. In this book Robert gives great perspectives and advice to start a backfire that may save your organization. Not only is this a great book for employees, but for bosses who think they are all alone."

Tim McDermott Chief Operating Officer, Praise FM

"With *Dear Employee* Robert McFarland has done it again. The author of *Dear Boss* has completed the cycle by giving insight into how employees can engage in Self-Leadership and enhance their work experience and the contribution they make at work as a result. In an age where there is often a disconnect between management and the labor force, building an effective team between the two is essential for flourishing. This book will help you get there from wherever you sit in your job."

Dr. Darrell L. Bock Executive Director for Cultural Engagement, Howard G. Hendricks Center for Christian Leadership and Cultural Engagement Senior Research Professor of New Testament Studies, Dallas Theological Seminary

"We've all had the frustrating experience of getting stuck in a vehicle. Often, the answer to getting out of a muddy rut is not to keep stepping on the accelerator, spinning the tires faster and going nowhere. Often, it takes a strategy and power to tow or push the car out. Help is here! If you feel that you're spinning your wheels on your career path, Robert lends a hand (and a plan!) with this book to get you unstuck and on your way again."

Dr. Jennifer Epperson Director of Research and Learning, Moody Radio

"I recommend this book to anyone dissatisfied with their job. Through biblical wisdom and years of practical business experience, Robert McFarland teaches strategies to pursue desired careers then helps the reader develop tools necessary to achieve them. This book is a valuable resource for job seekers as well as anyone interested in moving up the corporate ladder."

Debra Fraser President/CEO, Total Living International

"In *Dear Employee: What Your Boss Wishes You Knew*, Robert McFarland refreshingly and deftly breaks down the seemingly complex world of business management into simple to understand, bite size pieces of dealing with the human factor in the marketplace. Ultimately, it is all about Self-Leadership. This book can serve as a practical primer for those in positions of leadership to share with their employees as an effective starting point to discuss their work and the workplace environment. I recommend it!"

Joe Battaglia Broadcaster, author of *Unfriended: Finding True Community in a Disconnected Culture* President, Renaissance Communications

"In his book, *Dear Employee: What Your Boss Wishes You Knew*, Robert McFarland brilliantly blends business smarts with biblical truths. Most important to me, Robert enables readers to take action. Knowing the right thing to do is easier than doing the right thing. Robert's thoughtful approach will motivate every employee—and even their bosses—to do the right thing. Robert's solution of Self-Leadership, and his deep explanation on this solution, is one I totally endorse and share with professionals, friends, and family. I wanted to list the specific points I really liked in this endorsement—but the list got too long!"

Ben Case Chief Executive Officer, Focused On Fundraising, Inc.

"We live in a culture where complaining is almost a default response to any kind of stress. That's never healthy, but in the workplace, that can be toxic. Robert McFarland has already given us great insight into what employers need to hear from those they supervise. He's now helping us understand what employees need to know about their bosses. Respectful dialog, rather than corrosive complaint, is a key to resolution, productivity, and workplace satisfaction. McFarland charts a clear course toward that desirable end."

Robert F. Schwarzwalder, Jr. Director, Center for Christian Thought & Action, Regent University

"Robert McFarland did it again. His comprehensive work on *Dear Employee: What Your Boss Wishes you Knew* is an excellent work that will take leaders to a new level and bring upcoming leaders to new awareness of growth. Robert shows the reader not only his knowledge, but his experience comes out in this writing as well. The reader will be blessed in the reading."

Barbara Lachance CEO, Generational Solutions LLC

"Robert does an amazing job of breaking down and explaining what a boss goes through in running a business or organization. Once an employee understands the boss's role, it makes their job much easier. It makes them a better employee. This is a must read for every employee!"

Nathan Tabor nathantabor.com

"Robert McFarland has written an amazing book. If you employ people, you will find it helpful in communicating with your employees. If you are an employee, it will help you understand how your boss thinks and what he expects of you."

Steve Wingfield Founder and CEO, VICTORY WEEKEND Ministries
Partner, Lodestar-Guidance

"He's done it again! My longtime friend Robert McFarland wisely combines the timeless truths of scripture with tough and relevant questions. Read it with a teachable heart and an open mind to be challenged, encouraged, and taken to the next level. A must read for every boss and employee."

Stu Epperson, Jr. Founder/President, The Truth Network
Author, *First Words of Jesus: From the Cradle to the Cross*

DEAR EMPLOYEE
What Your Boss
Wishes You Knew

Robert McFarland

Published by Best Seller Publishing

Emphasis in Scripture shown by italics is the author's.

Unless otherwise indicated, Scripture quotations are from the ESV® Bible (The Holy Bible, English Standard Version®), copyright © 2001 by Crossway, a publishing ministry of Good News Publishers. Used by permission. All rights reserved.

Scripture quotations identified MSG are from *The Message* by Eugene H. Peterson, copyright © 1993, 1994, 1995, 2000, 2001, 2002. Used by permission of NavPress Publishing Group. All rights reserved.

Edited by Catherine McFarland, Christianna McFarland, Corally Wolters, and Ellyse Zou

Cover Design by Steve Fata
Interior layout design by BSP

ISBN 978-1-795134-22-4

To the Lord GOD,
Who gave me the inspiration for this book
and the perseverance to complete it.

To Tamitha, my beloved,
Thank you for believing in me
throughout this whole process.

Acknowledgments

To Tamitha: Thank you for being there with me throughout the writing process. I don't know how I would have completed this book without you.

To my wonderful children: Thank you for your taking an interest in my writing and encouraging me in getting this book done.

To all my clients: Thank you for inspiring me with your desire to become better than you are now through your Self-Leadership.

To Catherine, Christy, Corally, and Ellyse: Thank you for being brutally honest with me about this manuscript. Your editing abilities helped to polish this book into what it is.

To the WPA team: Thank you for helping me gather the research data I needed to write this book.

To my Lord GOD: Thank you for the inspiration for this book and for leading me to write it. May you receive all the glory from its publication.

Contents

Introduction

*"Even the most analytical thinkers are predictably irrational;
the really smart ones acknowledge and address
their irrationalities."*

—Dan Ariely

I was in a tough spot. I was in a job that was a bad fit for me, but I didn't realize it. People had warned me before taking the job that Mike was a tough guy to work for. I had smiled condescendingly and naively dismissed their concerns. That made for a miserable three months.

I had been tapped to be the executive director of a tiny but influential nonprofit. The title of the job impressed me, but I was in way over my head. And to make matters worse, I found myself incredibly intimidated by Mike.

While Mike was a tough boss, he was a fair man. He had a gentle and kind heart. He had high standards for himself, and he had high standards for others. He was not unreasonable in what he asked me to do. But I could not see that at the time, because I was not yet the person I am today.

Today I am interviewed about my books and my consultancy frequently. But back then, I got so nervous on camera that I could not remember what I was supposed to say during the interview.

Today I speak often in front of influential audiences. But back then, I was terrified to testify in front of a committee of the state legislature and could barely read my prepared testimony.

Today I hold people accountable as an executive coach. But back then, I put off keeping the inventory of Mike's books until I could no longer recall how many had shipped.

Use what your boss wishes you knew to become the person you want to become.

Today I counsel people in Self-Leadership to be mindful of their thoughts, words, and actions. But back then, I allowed for unhealthy outlets for my frustrations in the job.

Despite the fact that I was a poor fit for the job, I blamed Mike for the problems that I had at work. I wanted to justify myself so badly that I disregarded the reality of the situation. Instead I opted to look at the situation in a way that fit how I wanted to see myself.

Ultimately the situation reached a breaking point. Mike called me into his office and informed me that my employment there wasn't working out. He explained that my performance on the job was not up to his standard. But he also said my reactions to situations were not healthy. Although Mike was spot-on in his assessment, what was my response? I thought, "Good riddance! I don't need this anymore!"

It took me years to realize that I was in the wrong. But I am happy to say that I eventually did go to Mike and apologize for my actions. And Mike, being the good guy that he is, had long since forgiven and forgotten that episode.

Dan Ariely's quote at the start of this chapter sheds some light on that three-month ordeal. Even though I thought I was an analytical thinker, I was still prone to irrationality. In his book *Predictably Irrational*, Dr. Ariely explains that humans engage in actions and make decisions that are often divorced from rationality, and sometimes very far from ideal. Over the years I've tried to understand the silly, dumb, odd, amusing, and sometimes dangerous mistakes we all make, in the hope that by understanding our irrational quirks, we can retrain ourselves to make better decisions. ... The experiments my colleagues and I have conducted helped us discover why our participants (and humans in general, including ourselves) fail to reason properly.[1]

That's the way I was when I worked for Mike more than twenty years ago. I failed to reason properly, but I didn't ever think I was wrong. I didn't want to think that I *could* be wrong. But on a more basic level, I just didn't want to *think*. As Baylor Professor Alan Jacobs says in his book, *How to Think*, "we suffer from a settled determination to avoid thinking. Relatively few people *want* to think. Thinking troubles us; thinking tires us. Thinking can force us out of familiar, comforting habits."[2]

When I was in college, there was a time that thinking things through became very important. I had just started dating a new girlfriend. As she and I found out, we were very different. I was a social butterfly; she was an introvert. I liked hard rock music; she liked a softer sound. I was at the center of my world; Jesus was at the center of hers.

When we talked, she told me that she thought of herself as a sinful person and that she was in need of a savior. I told her I thought I was a pretty good person. I was glad that Jesus meant so much to her, but I was fine with the way my life was. That is, until my twenty-first birthday.

The day I turned twenty-one, my college friends determined that they wanted to help me celebrate. I don't even remember all that they gave me to drink that night. From what I remember of that evening—walking out in front of headlights, and hugging the toilet—I think I am fortunate to be alive today.

That night surprised me, and it surprised my girlfriend. Until then, she didn't realize I had a party lifestyle. And until then, I didn't realize how empty the party lifestyle made me feel.

That evening was a defining moment for me. It made me aware of an inconsistency in my life. I realized I wasn't as fulfilled by the party lifestyle as I thought I was—especially as my girlfriend was a lot happier with Jesus than I was at parties.

Five days later, I found myself sitting in the library at one of the study carrels. I realized I had a decision to make: keep going on as I had been, or do something with the information I now had about myself. I could either ignore this information, or be responsible with this information. I needed to think.

After thinking a lot that day, I said, "If you're there, God, I need to do something different. There's got to be something better than this." As a result of that thinking on November 17, 1988, I made a choice to follow Jesus. (Almost exactly two years later, I asked that young woman to be my wife. Tamitha and I are still married today.)

Over the thirty years I have been following Jesus, I have realized that the Scripture says it is important *that* we think (Psalm 119:59; 2 Corinthians 10:5). In addition, the Bible talks about the importance of *how* we think (Romans 12:3; 1 Corinthians 8:2; Galatians 6:3).

I particularly enjoy Dr. Jacobs' definition of thinking. In *How to Think*, he describes this practice as *"the power to be finely aware and richly responsible. We just need to learn how to be more aware, how to act more responsibly."*[3]

It is my hope that this book will help you be more aware of yourself and how to be more responsible with your situation at work. As a result, I hope that you will use what your boss wishes you knew to become the person you want to become.

In the process of becoming that person, realize that you might not currently have a full understanding of the real situation at your workplace. Just like when I was working for Mike, you may have contributed to the problems you see at work. You must take responsibility for your actions. And you can choose to initiate the change you want to see in yourself.

Instead of doing what I did working with Mike, it is important for you to look at how you see yourself. Even if you are not the leader of the company, you are the leader of yourself.

I have coached many people in leading themselves through personal and professional challenges. I tell my clients that self-leadership always precedes team leadership: you must be able to effectively lead yourself before you can effectively lead others. (To access more resources and get your questions answered, visit www.WhatYourBossWishesYouKnew.com.)

To help you navigate your career, this book offers a solution: Self-Leadership. This way of thinking is designed to help you become a person of HOPE (Honoring, Open, Perceptive, and Engaged) by changing how you see yourself and the world. By changing how you see yourself, Self-Leadership will transform you from the inside out through what you think, say, do, and permit. By changing the way you see the world, Self-Leadership holds the promise of transforming your career.

Reflection Questions

1. How self-aware are you? How much are you willing to take responsibility for yourself?

2. When have you become aware that you were oblivious to your blind spots?

3. How often do you take time to reflect on the part you play in the workplace problems you see?

Notes
[1] Dan Ariely, *Predictably Irrational: The Hidden Forces That Shape Our Decisions* (New York: Harper, 2009), xi, xii.

[2] Alan Jacobs, *How to Think: A Survival Guide for a World at Odds* (New York: Currency, 2017), 17.

[3] Ibid, 49.

PART I
A VIEW FROM
THE CORNER OFFICE

Part One discusses the scope of the research survey and explains the results. Chapter One provides the background for the survey and the demographic breakdown of the participants. Chapters Two through Five discuss the four dominant themes from the research by analyzing three representative responses in each chapter.

Chapter 1:   **The Research Survey and Its Findings**
In this national survey, I asked an open-ended question: *What would you say is the one thing you wish employees that report to you knew that they might not already know?* The responses fell into four major themes.

Chapter 2:   **Theme #1 – Insufficient Acknowledgement**
Bosses do not feel their employees understand nor appreciate what they do for them. They feel

employees do not respect the managerial role bosses occupy, nor sufficiently support their bosses.

Chapter 3:   **Theme #2 – Imperfect Communication**
Bosses believe employees need to communicate better with them. Bosses do not think they get sufficient information in a timely manner from their employees, nor do they feel they are getting the whole story.

Chapter 4:   **Theme #3 – Incomplete Picture**
Bosses are concerned their employees do not accurately perceive nor understand what goes on at the workplace, what their bosses have to do, nor how employees should do their jobs.

Chapter 5:   **Theme #4 – Inadequate Ethic**
Bosses do not believe their employees work hard enough on the job. They do not think employees show up on time, take enough ownership of their jobs, nor work together as a team.

Why It Matters

The research results provide quantitative and qualitative data you can use to understand how your boss thinks. By understanding what your boss might be thinking, you can learn how to use that insight to your advantage.

CHAPTER 1

The Research Survey and Its Findings

"Research is to see what everybody else has seen,
and to think what nobody else has thought.
—Albert Szent-Gyorgyi

At my first job, I heard employees complaining about their bosses. They would gripe among themselves about what management was doing. And whenever anything went wrong, they were quick to place the blame with management.

- They complained about all that management did wrong. In fact, they didn't limit their comments to the boss's performance; they also assessed the boss's motives and intelligence. They often determined among themselves that their bosses were not just incompetent, but insensitive and stupid as well.

- They thought that they weren't told what was really going on at the workplace. They didn't feel like they were getting the straight story and they believed that management was withholding important information from them. As a result, they were not sure that they could trust their bosses.

- They said that their bosses didn't realize their management plans had unintended consequences. They said that their bosses didn't understand what their employees' jobs entailed or what their employees had to deal with in working with customers. And they wondered what the bosses were doing all day while they were the ones doing the *real* work.

- They tended to complain about the work they were assigned. They felt like they were being told to do things that they shouldn't have to do. They pointed out that their job encroached too much on their personal time. And they didn't want to be the only ones working when their colleagues weren't doing their fair share.

Over nearly thirty years I have seen the same perspectives in virtually every business, nonprofit organization, and even ministry. At the same time though, there are two sides to every story. While management is responsible for leading their employees well, every employee is responsible for responding appropriately. And employees may miss the mark in what they should do just as often as managers may miss the mark in what they should do.

> *While management is responsible for leading their employees well, every employee is responsible for responding appropriately.*

This book will explore what your boss wishes you knew using research as a starting point and Scripture as a road map. This book blends business smarts with biblical wisdom to help you use these insights to thrive at work. Each chapter will contain Reflection Questions for immediate use and Scripture references for further study. And throughout this book I will be direct with my words: I don't want you to have to lose as much time as I did in getting around to taking responsibility for yourself.

To gather the data for this book, I commissioned WPA Opinion Research[1] in the fall of 2016 to conduct a research survey of 589 U.S. adults.[2] Fifty-four percent of them were male, and 46 percent were female. Regionally, 35 percent were in the South, 23 percent were in the Midwest, 22 percent were in the West, and 20 percent were in the Northeast. In terms of age, 34 percent were 18 to 34 years old, 22 percent were 35 to 44, 22 percent were 45 to 54, 16 percent were 55 to 64, and 6 percent were over 65. (I also asked about their race, total household income, education level, and household size. The responses to those questions can be found in Appendix A.)

In addition to these demographic questions, I also asked some questions about their work.

Which of the following best describes where you fit in your organization?

I own the business or am part of the senior management team.	12%
I both report to someone above me and have people who directly report to me.	25%
I perform a specific job and report to someone about that work.	48%
I'm not sure/none of these.	15%

I also asked what kind of work they did.

In what industry would you say you work?

Health Care and Social Assistance	11%
Retail Trade	10%
Educational Services	9%

Manufacturing	8%
Professional, Scientific, and Technical Services	8%
Transportation and Warehousing	7%
Finance and Insurance	5%
Accommodation and Food Services	5%
Construction	4%
Local Government	4%
Information Services	3%
Federal Government	3%
Wholesale Trade	2%
Utilities	2%
Real Estate and Rental and Leasing	2%
Arts, Entertainment, and Recreation	2%
State Government	2%
Agriculture, Forestry, Fishing, and Hunting	1%
Mining, Quarrying, and Oil and Gas Extraction	1%
Management of Companies and Enterprises	1%
Other	5%
I'm not sure	5%

I then asked an open-ended question of the 37 percent who said they had employees reporting to them. To refocus the participants in the study on the question at hand, I framed the question within the context of the communication they have with their employees.

When you think about how you interact with employees, and all the formal and informal communication that occurs, what would you say is the one thing you wish employees that report to you knew that they might not already know?

The typed answers were then collected and analyzed. Other than those who did not respond or were not sure what to say, the vast majority of answers fell into four categories.

Acknowledgement	**17%**
Communication	**15%**
Work Ethic	**14%**
Big Picture	**12%**
Other	4%
Nothing	34%
I'm not sure	3%

The numbers do not tell the whole story. The verbatim responses themselves provide a better picture of how these bosses perceive the employees they work with. One boss said "that the job must be done whether they like to do it or not[;] that's what they are paid to do." Another boss said "How much I appreciate them." Still another boss said "how much of an active protective barricade I [c]ontinuously actively provide for them, in regards to the person I report to. I protect them from him."

Some of the bosses had responses that were enlightened, and some did not. But that doesn't matter. You can learn from good bosses, and you can learn from bad ones. What matters is whether you will allow them to teach you.

Now, you might say, "But you don't know my boss!" And I would likely have to agree. I probably don't know your boss. But it doesn't matter who your boss is. It doesn't

You cannot demand that others change if you are not willing to change. The change you want to see in others first has to start with you.

matter whether your boss is a good guy or a bad guy. Deserved or not, bad things will happen to you. What matters is how you respond to them; what ultimately matters is your attitude.

Chuck Swindoll, the senior pastor of Stonebriar Community Church in Frisco, Texas, and the voice for the *Insight for Living* broadcast, said this about attitude.

> The longer I live, the more I realize the impact of attitude on life. Attitude, to me, is more important than facts. It is more important than the past, than education, than money, than circumstances, than failure, than successes, than what other people think or say or do. It is more important than appearance, giftedness or skill. It will make or break a company ... a church ... a home. The remarkable thing is we have a choice everyday regarding the attitude we will embrace for that day. We cannot change our past ... we cannot change the fact that people will act in a certain way. We cannot change the inevitable. The only thing we can do is play on the one string we have, and that is our attitude. I am convinced that life is 10% what happens to me and 90% of how I react to it. And so it is with you ... we are in charge of our Attitudes.[3]

You will benefit the most from reading about this research if you can look at the survey responses without preconceived bias. I hope you will see what you can learn from these statements instead of finding ways to say that they don't apply to you.

If you assume a position of humility and are willing to be taught by these survey respondents, then you may see yourself—and your boss—in a new light. You cannot demand that others change if you are not willing to change. The change you want to see in others first has to start with you.

Reflection Questions

1. How would you describe your attitude?

2. Are there any unresolved issues between you and your boss?

3. How could you help resolve those issues?

Notes

[1] Now rebranded as WPA Intelligence.

[2] This research was conducted online. Multiple online panels were used in the construction of the sample to avoid bias from any one specific panel. The sample included business owners, managers, and employees in a wide variety of industries and ensured representation of gender, geography, education, income, race/ethnicity, and age. The data were gathered September 8-12, 2016, in accordance with industry best practices and standards.

[3] https://www.goodreads.com/quotes/267482-the-longer-i-live-the-more-i-realize-the-impact, accessed September 12, 2018.

CHAPTER 2

Theme #1
Insufficient Acknowledgement

"Every man … wants to be recognized."

—Albert Camus

When I got the initial shipment of my first book, *Dear Boss: What Your Employees Wish You Knew*, I was giddy about holding a copy of the book in my hand. Writing the book took a long time, and I was glad to finally see the fruits of my labor. But I also realized many other people had helped me get my book to this point, and I wanted to thank them for their part. I sent copies to those who had helped me in getting it published: my family, my friends, my developmental editor, the endorsers of the book, and those who were listed in the acknowledgements. I received reactions of gratitude from most people, but I was particularly struck by the reaction of those who were listed in the acknowledgements. I wondered if they were as giddy about being listed in the acknowledgements as I was about holding the book in my hand.

Being acknowledged and appreciated is not limited to the people on my acknowledgements page. All people desire to be acknowledged and appreciated. A mother appreciates a child bringing her a flower to thank her for being a mom. A coach appreciates a player giving a shout out for all the time devoted to improve performance. And a boss appreciates the team acknowledging what he or she did to guide and lead the team.

> *All people desire to be acknowledged and appreciated.*

Seventeen percent of the bosses who responded to the survey said how important acknowledgement was to them. Within that context, below are three representative responses to the open-ended question, "What would you say is the one thing you wish employees that report to you knew that they might not already know?"

1. How good they have it

This comment by one of the survey respondents provides an important perspective. While society may deem that it is better to be the boss, there are responsibilities that are associated with that position. Not having those responsibilities can be seen as a blessing (Ecclesiastes 5:12).

Apparently this boss has people who work for her who do not fully appreciate their job or their boss. Not appreciating the boss's role can hurt their future at the company—and their relationship with the boss.

Not fully knowing what your boss has to deal with can skew your understanding of what your boss does. As a result, you may think the grass is greener on the other side, when it might not really be.

2. don't forget I'm boss

This response to the survey emphasizes an important ability the boss has—to hire and fire. Apparently this respondent has to deal with employees who do not respect the boss's role. Not recognizing the boss's role can make for an uncomfortable situation with the boss. And being oblivious or uncaring about the possibility of being fired is a dangerous place to be. No one is irreplaceable, regardless if they are an entry-level worker or the chief executive.

3. I'm working hard for them

This survey respondent wants his employees to know how hard he works for them. Apparently they may disregard his efforts or they may not be aware of what he does for them. Either way, they would do well to acknowledge how he is working on their behalf.

This boss seems to be a supportive boss who is concerned about the people working for him, and he seems to want them to have that same level of support for his efforts. Working for the benefit of his employees while not having their support can become a frustrating endeavor.

This survey response suggests that you are not the only one working hard. Your boss may well be working hard too, even if it does not appear that way from your vantage point.

This research has shown that not all employees acknowledge the authority over them—and there can be consequences for that lack of acknowledgement. In Scripture, John rebukes Diotrephes because he "does not acknowledge our authority" and instead "likes to put himself first" (3 John 9). That self-centered attitude will not put anyone in good stead with the one(s) they report to.

Demonstrating appreciation of others is powerful, as I found with the people on my acknowledgements page. You will do well to acknowledge what your bosses do on your behalf.

Reflection Questions

1. Do you see your situation in any of the survey responses?

2. How much do you acknowledge what your boss does for you?

3. Is there anything you think you should change about yourself? If so, how?

CHAPTER 3

Theme #2
Imperfect Communication

*"The most important thing in communication
is hearing what isn't said."*

—Peter Drucker

Several years ago, I offered my assistant a high profile assignment. Because she was good at interfacing with our customers, I wanted her to participate in a significant event in Los Angeles where many of our best customers would attend. I knew that she would represent the organization well, and I thought she would enjoy the event since she knew many of the people already. But to my surprise, she declined with no explanation. I assumed she declined because it would have required her to fly across the country and be away from home for the better part of a week, so I didn't question her about it.

When we were going to host another similar event in Washington, D.C., I offered her the opportunity to attend, expecting her to say yes. Many of the same people that she knew well would be in attendance, and I knew that she would be a great asset to the organization in that role. The event was only an hour from where she lived, so she could drive back home each night if she wanted to. But again she declined with no explanation.

This time I wanted more information. I was confused as to why she didn't want to attend. I was concerned that her lack of interest signified a deeper problem. When I asked her why she did not want to participate, she surprised me with her answer. She said that she did not like to drive, and the idea of driving in Los Angeles in a rental car—or even driving her own car into Washington, D.C.—really scared her. When I understood the root issue, I was then able to make

> *By communicating directly, honestly and transparently, you can be a part of the solution at your workplace— and not part of the confusion.*

accommodations for her to participate in future events. As I predicted, she performed admirably at every event.

Workplace communication can often be misunderstood or misinterpreted. When I was trying to communicate with my assistant, we had two different perceptions. I thought I was offering a prized assignment, but she interpreted it as a terrifying ordeal. She was reluctant to share that she did not like to drive, so I suspected there were deeper problems that needed to be resolved. As a result, we did not have open communication.

Similarly, 15 percent of the bosses who responded to the survey said that communication was their most important concern with employees. Within that context, here are three representative responses to the question, "What would you say is the one thing you wish employees that report to you knew that they might not already know?"

1. How to say what they need
This boss seems to want to help his employees, but they seem reluctant to let him for whatever reason. They apparently are not forthcoming about what they need in order to do their job, and he is therefore unable to remedy the situation. If this boss is genuinely trying to solicit what they need, then these employees should be straightforward in telling him.

It could also be that this boss wants his direct reports to be cognizant of *how* to say what they need. It's possible that they are not sharing their concerns in a helpful way. In that case, what they are saying could sound like complaining rather than requesting.

Without open communication, workplace interaction is compromised. Just like in the story I related about my assistant, your boss is not able to improve your work situation if your communication is not forthcoming. Communication has never been—nor can ever be—a one-way street.

2. That I can tell when they are lying
This respondent is warning his employees that he thinks he knows when they are not telling the truth. Something is tipping him off that they are not being truthful. It is also possible that he is incorrect about them lying. He may be misinterpreting something they are doing or saying, and therefore believing something about them that is not true.

Regardless, the statement this boss makes should encourage you to maintain your integrity. While it may be tempting to make an untruthful statement in order to deflect criticism or get the boss off your back, it is never a good idea to lie, regardless if you are a front-line employee or a CEO. Honesty is still the best policy, because it is likely that a lie will find you out (Luke 8:17).

3. how to communicate effectively
This survey response seems to indicate that this boss wants to improve the effectiveness of his employees' communication, but it is unknown whether his employees understand or appreciate that.

Clear communication helps both parties. Even if your boss is not a good communicator, you can take the initiative. Providing a transparent foundation for free-flowing communication helps your boss better understand your perspective.

Communication is crucial for any enterprise to succeed. It is imperative for everyone to be on the same page—as my assistant and I discovered. By communicating directly, honestly and transparently (Matthew 5:37), you can be a part of the solution at your workplace— and not part of the confusion.

Reflection Questions

1. On a scale of 1-10, how good a communicator do you think you are? Why do you think so?

2. Do you see your situation in any of the survey responses?

3. Is there anything you think should be changed about your communication techniques? In what way(s)?

CHAPTER 4

Theme #3
Incomplete Picture

"If you just focus on the smallest details,
you never get the big picture right."

—Leroy Hood

George Seurat painted a pointillist masterpiece known as *A Sunday Afternoon on the Island of La Grande Jatte*. The painting is an enormous work of art, measuring nearly 7 feet tall and more than 10 feet long, depicting nineteenth century French society relaxing on the banks of the Seine River, near the city center of Paris. Other than its large size, the painting may not seem particularly noteworthy to the uninitiated art critic—like myself—except when looked at up close.

At close range, you will notice it is entirely composed of little dots. The artist employed no blended brush strokes, only small dots of paint, to create the visual effect. Seurat placed the dots of color closely next to others to create each perceived hue. As a result, he made the human eye do the work of blending the colors, instead of his paint brush.[1]

This painting illustrates what happens when you look too closely at a situation. As with Seurat's famous work, if you do not pull back and see the big picture, you end up missing what is really going on. By focusing on the little dots, you don't see that they come together to produce a much more complex image. At your workplace, if you allow yourself to look too closely at your particular situation, you miss seeing how your job is part of a much more complex scene.

The research survey showed that 12 percent of bosses said they wanted their employees to be accurately perceiving what they see at the workplace. Within that context, here are three representative responses to the question, "What would you say is the one thing you wish employees that report to you knew that they might not already know?"

1. How their job fits into the overall organization.
This respondent may be frustrated that his direct reports do not understand that the things they do matter in the grand scheme of the organization. He may be concerned that they don't see how important their work is.

It could also be that this respondent wants those who report to him to see how the work they do impacts everyone else in the organization. It could be that he wants these employees to change their perspective of their own role so they can become more aware of how they could contribute to the success of the company.

Regardless of the reasoning behind this response, the statement is still helpful. It is important for you to understand how your job fits into the overall organization. While management bears a responsibility to explain that perspective within the organization, it is incumbent on you to embrace it.

2. [It's] easier to do it the right way than to take short cuts doing it the wrong way

This survey response illustrates the frustration of a boss who has had to correct employees who have decided to work outside of the company standards. The results of those decisions can be costly: time wasted from having to redo work as a result of "short-cuts," lost productivity from having to clean up the problems caused by "doing it the wrong way," and efforts expended by management to retrain those employees so they can "do it the right way."

If you allow yourself to look too closely at your particular situation, you miss seeing how your job is part of a much more complex scene.

This boss also appears to wish that her employees would realize that *avoiding* the short-cuts is actually the "easier" way. She understands that the company way will actually make everyone's job easier.

It's crucial to understand that management has set forward a "right way" to do things. Perhaps you may find a short-cut that you believe to be better, but it should be submitted to management for evaluation. There may be unrealized and unintended consequences from short-cuts; that's why you should be willing to understand and appreciate proper procedure.

3. They are the face of the company and our 1st impression to our customers

This survey respondent seems to believe that her employees do not realize the significant role they have in representing the company.

They don't seem to realize how important they are to the company's reputation with their customer base.

While managers have the responsibility to train employees in how to represent the company, every employee has the responsibility to embrace representing the company. A front-line employee may directly interface more often with customers, but every employee— including the CEO—has at least some customer interaction.

As an employee, it's important to understand the influence your interactions have on current and future customers. Anything you do internally can externally impact customer relationships.

Like George Seurat's pointillist masterpiece, there is a bigger picture than what you can see from your perspective, regardless of your role (Isaiah 55:8-9). By expanding your perspective, you will perceive the significance of that role.

Reflection Questions

1.   How does your job fit into the overall organization?

2.   Do you see your situation in any of the survey responses?

3.   How significant do you believe your role is at your workplace?

Notes
_____

[1]   http://www.webexhibits.org/colorart/jatte.html, accessed November 21, 2018.

CHAPTER 5

Theme #4
Inadequate Ethic

*"I can only control myself, my actions,
my work ethic, and my attitude."*

—Ali Krieger

Many years ago, I worked for a government agency which had a bad organizational culture. Many of the civil servants had an entitled attitude toward their jobs. They did not work hard; they just coasted along. Because firing non-performers was problematic, those who didn't have a good work ethic never left. And yet, when it came time for performance evaluations, they received outstanding reviews from their supervisors.

One award ceremony proved memorable to me. The division was presenting wood plaques to the award recipients. Going into the award ceremony, the honorees knew they were going to receive "a piece of the wood" for an outstanding performance review without having performed outstanding work. No one was excited about their awards. No one was grateful for their awards. No one really cared about them at all.

Like those government agency employees, the believers in the early church of Thessalonica did not have a good picture of the importance of work. The Apostle Paul felt it necessary to give instructions to the Thessalonian church about how to deal with people who did not have a good work ethic. In his second letter to the Thessalonians, Paul said that he, Silvanus, and Timothy gave them "an example to imitate" because "we were not idle when we were with you, nor did we eat anyone's bread without paying for it, but with toil and labor we worked night and day, that we might not be a burden to any of you" (2 Thessalonians 3:7-9).

> *The value system that someone brings to their work defines the quality of work they will produce.*

A good work ethic is as important now as it was then, but it can still be just as hard to find, like in that government agency I worked for. The value system that someone brings to their work defines the quality of work they will produce.

Fourteen percent of the surveyed bosses said the ethic their employees applied to their work was important. Regarding that work ethic, here are three representative responses to the question, "What would you say is the one thing you wish employees that report to you knew that they might not already know?"

1. ... if they show up and do their work we won't have issues.
This respondent may be referring to employees who habitually do not show up. This boss seems to have employees who have made it a habit to call in (or maybe they don't even do that) to say that they will not be coming in. If that's the case, then they have soured the relationship with their boss.

It could also be that she is referring to the famous Woody Allen quote: "Eighty percent of success is showing up." Perhaps she is frustrated that employees do not show up prepared to work. They may be physically present but mentally checked out. Or it could be that *showing up* and *working* represents what she believes is expected of them, and they are not living up to her expectations. Regardless of the scenario, her employees apparently did not really "show up" and therefore they are not really there to "do their work."

> *By showing up and being a team player, you will cultivate the reputation you want.*

As a result of not showing up to work, there are consequences—or as she calls them, "issues"—for their lack of dedication. These employees would do well to understand what her expectations are so that they will not invite these "issues" upon themselves.

2. we are all part of the team

This respondent may be making a statement about the morale of the workplace, but it is unclear whether that statement is positive or negative. It could be that this boss is making a declarative statement about how good the team environment is where she works and she is exulting in the fact that she has a great team. On the flip side, it could be that she is making an emphatic statement, venting about the need for a team-based approach among her employees.

Regardless of which scenario is correct, the statement is nonetheless accurate. As I said in my first book, *Dear Boss: What Your Employees Wish You Knew*, "everyone on the team can make a difference for the overall success of the team, and everyone on the team is dependent on everyone else on the team."[1] How you view yourself in relation to everyone else is important to the overall health of the organization.

3. how to be responsible, how to be curious, how to take their job seriously
This respondent seems to be frustrated with her employees for not taking ownership of their situation. At the same time, she might not be complaining, but instead giving some sage advice: take responsibility for your actions on the job.

In fact, it sounds like she is expecting her employees to think like managers, even if her employees are not managers. Regardless, this boss has given some good counsel to her employees for how they can be prepared for management, even if they currently are not there yet.

This research demonstrated that not all employees appear to have a good work ethic. As Paul warned in his second letter to the Thessalonians, you would be wise to "keep away from [anyone] who is walking in idleness, ... to do [your] work quietly and to earn [your] own living" (2 Thessalonians 3:6, 12). By showing up and being a team player, you will cultivate the reputation you want.

Reflection Questions

1. How would you characterize your work ethic?

2. Do you see your situation in any of the survey responses?

3. Is there anything you think you should change about your work ethic? In what way?

Notes

[1] Robert McFarland, *Dear Boss: What Your Employees Wish You Knew* (Pasadena: Best Seller Publishing, 2017), 109.

PART II
SELF-LEADERSHIP

In Part Two, we will explore Self-Leadership as a means of addressing what your boss wishes you knew. Self-Leadership is the process of becoming intentionally aware of yourself and taking responsibility for your thoughts, words, and actions.

Chapter 6:   **The Need for Self-Leadership**
Wherever your career is right now, be willing to change how you look at yourself. Shifting your paradigm will allow you to see yourself from a different vantage point.

Chapters 7-10:   **Paradigm Shift #1 – Honoring**
Respect the position that your boss holds, even if you do not think your boss deserves that honor. You should also express your appreciation and support for what your boss does for you.

Chapters 11-14: Paradigm Shift #2 – Open

Have open communication with your boss. This means not only being honest with your boss, but also freely sharing information in a timely manner.

Chapters 15-18: Paradigm Shift #3 – Perceptive

Try to see the big picture in the organization. Look beyond yourself and see how what you do affects everyone else—especially when it comes to interfacing with customers.

Chapters 19-22: Paradigm Shift #4 – Engaged

Recognize that employees and management are two parts of the same team. As an employee, you must work hard on the job and be self-motivated. You must hold yourself to the same standard you hold your boss to.

Why It Matters

By making these four paradigm shifts, from "business as usual" to a Self-Leadership model, you can transform your outlook and become a person of HOPE (Honoring, Open, Perceptive, and Engaged).

CHAPTER 6

The Need for Self-Leadership

"you know far less about yourself than you feel you do."
—Daniel Kahneman

Our society today has a self-leadership crisis. It doesn't matter where we look—business, politics, entertainment—we see its effects. The news regularly reports about the financial improprieties of business executives. Politicians get caught all the time doing something they knew they should not do. And the grocery store tabloid headlines are always proclaiming how such and such movie star is cheating on so-and-so.

We see people in positions of authority at our workplaces doing things that we think are ill-informed at best and malicious at worst. We see people around us making poor choices that are out of our control and we shake our heads, saying we would do things differently if given the choice. It seems like everyone around us has lost their mind—everyone except ourself, of course.

But perhaps we are not so immune from making poor choices as we might think. As Dan Ariely tells us in his book *Predictably Irrational,*

"Even good people are not immune to being partially blinded by their own minds."[1] Dr. Ariely goes on to explain that "we are pawns in a game whose forces we largely fail to comprehend. We usually think of ourselves as sitting in the driver's seat, with ultimate control over the decisions we make and the direction our life takes; but, alas, this perception has more to do with our desires—with how we want to view ourselves—than with reality."[2]

The choices we make today are influenced by the choices we have made before, even if they were poor choices. This is due in no small part to what Dr. Ariely calls *self-herding*. "This happens when we believe something is good (or bad) on the basis of our own previous behavior."[3] Dr. Ariely explains that doing something beforehand paves the way for us to do it again. If we do it a second time, that reinforces the decision to do it a third time—simply because we have done it twice before. Using the example of seeing people standing in line for a restaurant, Dr. Ariely explains that we perceive the restaurant must be good because people are lining up to get inside. The decision to go to that restaurant is validated simply because others want to go there. The restaurant decision is similar to making any kind of decision: "once we become the first person in line at the restaurant, we begin to line up behind ourself in subsequent experiences."[4] We do things again simply because we have done them before.

As we unwittingly become entrenched in our own opinions, we also become more resistant to changing our minds. Dr. Bridget Queenan, associate director of the Brain Initiative at the University of California at Santa Barbara, finds that humans like knowing what they know and don't want to be confused with the facts. "You have instincts for fight and for flight, not so much for insight. ... When people are threatened in any way, they retreat from logic. ... Little kids are perfectly capable of updating their belief systems and behaviors based on evidence. In fact, they find new and contradictory things really appealing. So why do *we* stop?"[5]

We stop updating our belief systems at least in part because of *heuristics*. Heuristics are mental short-cuts we use to make decisions. Instead of having to evaluate every single decision every single day—such as what we will eat or wear—we tend to use heuristics to avoid having to consider all the potential options available to us.

Unfortunately, heuristics can also extend to decisions we make at the workplace. When we come to our conclusions, we stick with them, and we don't want to be bothered with revisiting them. Once we have made up our minds, we assume that we can't be wrong. As a result, we stick with our opinions that have now become comforting and self-validating.

When we don't know how to reconcile our opinions with the reality around us—like I did when I worked for Mike—we assume that something "out there" is to blame. But we should consider whether we should stick with our paradigm—how we have always looked at the world—or if we need to make a paradigm shift. When we shift our paradigm, we begin to allow our minds to look at things differently.

As we unwittingly become entrenched in our own opinions, we also become more resistant to changing our minds.

I'm impressed that you have read this far. I realize that making yourself think differently may be a difficult process. But because you have read this far, I believe that you are capable of making those paradigm shifts.

Based on the research I conducted, bosses have four major predispositions, and these four predispositions will impact you at work.

1. Bosses do not feel their employees understand nor appreciate what they do for them. They feel employees do not respect the managerial role bosses occupy, nor sufficiently support their bosses.

2. Bosses believe employees need to communicate better with them. Bosses do not think they get sufficient information in a timely manner from their employees, nor do they feel they are getting the whole story.

3. Bosses are concerned their employees do not accurately perceive nor understand what goes on at the workplace, what their bosses have to do, nor how employees should do their jobs.

4. Bosses do not believe their employees work hard enough on the job. They do not think employees show up on time, take enough ownership of their jobs, nor work together as a team.

It doesn't have to be this way. In the rest of this section, you will read about Self-Leadership. And you may find that your Self-Leadership is more important than you realize.

Through the process of Self-Leadership, you can become the person you were created to be. Maybe your past is telling

> *Through the process of Self-Leadership, you can become the person you were created to be.*

you that you can't do something. Maybe the people in your life are telling you that you won't be more than you are now. Maybe your current scenario is making you feel hopeless. Regardless of where you are now, you can change. You can exercise Self-Leadership, and you can have HOPE. In unpacking Self-Leadership, we will discuss four themes.

1. Becoming HONORING of Your Boss
Respect the position that your boss holds, even if you do not think your boss deserves that honor. You should also express your appreciation and support for what your boss does for you.

2. Becoming OPEN with Your Boss
Have open communication with your boss. This means not only being honest with your boss, but also freely sharing information in a timely manner.

3. Becoming PERCEPTIVE of the Bigger Picture
Try to see the big picture in the organization. Look beyond yourself and see how what you do affects everyone else—especially when it comes to interfacing with customers.

4. Becoming ENGAGED at Work
Recognize that employees and management are two parts of the same team. As an employee, you must work hard on the job and be self-motivated. You must hold yourself to the same standard you hold your boss to.

Through exploring these four tenets of having HOPE—Honoring, Open, Perceptive, and Engaged—you will create a mindset that will give you the power to change your current situation. By actively working through these concepts, you can develop the self-awareness, the self-control, and the Self-Leadership to become a person of HOPE.

Reflection Questions

1. In what ways have you seen *self-herding* take place in your life? In your career?

2. In what ways have you seen *heuristics* in action in your life? In your career?

3. In what ways have you blamed "the system" for the situation you find yourself in?

Notes
_____

[1] Dan Ariely, *Predictably Irrational: The Hidden Forces That Shape Our Decisions* (New York: Harper, 2009), 227.

[2] Ibid, 243.

[3] Ibid, 37.

[4] Ibid.

[5] Joe Queenan, "Neuro-logic: How your brain is keeping you from changing your mind," *The Rotarian*, May 2018, 40, 43. Emphasis added.

CHAPTER 7

Paradigm Shift #1
Honoring

"Honor bespeaks worth."

—J.C. Penney

Many years ago I worked with a woman I'll call Phyllis. She was good at what she did. She knew how to get things done. And she had been around since our department was formed. In many ways, she was invaluable to the organization. But she did not show honor to our boss.

Phyllis' opposition to her boss was palpable. She felt strongly about her opinions. She knew she was right. That meant her boss had to be wrong. I remember many times she would march into our boss's office and shut the door. The rest of us could hear the two of them shouting through the closed door.

This confrontational situation had gone on for years before I arrived. About a year and a half after my hiring, the organization went through a financial crisis. Budgets got slashed and perks disappeared. And then management had to turn to layoffs. By many accounts,

Phyllis was the most essential employee in our department, but she was the only one our boss laid off.

After she was let go, the atmosphere in the office changed. We all noticed how the mood lifted without her there. My boss told me that he had dealt with Phyllis for so long that he knew how to deal with her, but he did not realize how her attitude affected the entire department. He said if he had understood how her departure would have impacted the organization, he would have fired her years earlier.

Phyllis didn't honor her boss, and it came back to bite her. She thought she was being helpful by being confrontational, but her dishonoring attitude poisoned the office dynamic and led to her firing.

> *Honoring someone else means you have to take your eyes off of yourself.*

Honoring someone else is not slavishly doing what they want. Honoring someone else means you have to take your eyes off of yourself. This doesn't mean that you are making yourself a doormat for someone else. You don't have to think less of yourself; you just have to think of yourself less.

Honor is a powerful force. When you honor other people, it affirms their humanity. It shows that you are willing to put them in a position of respect. The Apostle Paul put the issue of honor in its proper light when he explained that everyone in a position of authority was placed there by God. "Let every person be subject to the governing authorities. For there is no authority except from God, and those that exist have been instituted by God. ... Pay to all what is owed to them: ... respect to whom respect is owed, honor to whom honor is owed" (Romans 13:1, 7). It doesn't matter who the governing authorities are. It doesn't matter if they are good leaders or if they are bad leaders. The Scripture says that they should be honored simply because they are in a position of authority.

Now, you may say, "You don't know my boss!" As I've said before, I probably don't know your boss. But it doesn't matter. Your boss is worthy of honor simply because he or she has been placed in a position of authority—regardless if you believe your boss should be in that position or not.

In Chapter One, I quoted Chuck Swindoll: "I am convinced that life is 10% what happens to me and 90% of how I react to it." The only thing we can control is our attitude. If we choose to point to outside forces as the reason for our current situation, we then abdicate control over our lives. At that point, we can end up taking on a victim mentality. As Bob Hasson and Danny Silk say in their book, *The Business of Honor*, "When we feel powerless and are not taking responsibility for our lives, we look to other people to blame and manipulate."[1] Instead, we should adjust our attitude and take responsibility for what happens in our lives.

> *You cannot just point the finger at others to do their part. You have to be willing to do your part.*

Now, you may say that those who are in authority should be the ones to take the initiative to show honor. While I agree that management has a responsibility to their employees (which I share in my first book, *Dear Boss: What Your Employees Wish You Knew*), you still have a part to play in the process of changing the dynamic in your workplace. Again quoting Hasson and Silk, "Only by bringing honor to the table can we invite and expect others to reciprocate. Honor is not something we demand or require from others."[2] You cannot just point the finger at others to do their part. You have to be willing to do your part to honor others.

In this section, we will explore what Honoring looks like. In each chapter about Honoring—and in the subsequent chapters about how to be Open, Perceptive, and Engaged—I will pose a Self-Leadership question which ties the issue to a comment made by a survey respondent. In the next three chapters, we will explore the following three topics.

1. Appreciation
Express appreciation to your boss for what he or she does for you. You should appreciate your boss even if he or she doesn't appreciate you.

2. Respect
Get rid of any entitlement mentality. Recognize that your boss does not have to employ you. And respect your boss as an authority, even if you don't believe he or she deserves to be in that role.

3. Support
Be willing to do what is necessary to support the decisions your boss makes, even if you do not feel those decisions are the best ones.

It is my prayer that in the following chapters you will see how much you will personally benefit from honoring those in authority. And as you see your situation more clearly, I hope you will learn something from Phyllis' example—and implement what you learn.

Reflection Questions

1. How much do you appreciate your boss?

2. How much do you respect your boss?

3. How much do you support your boss?

Notes
___

[1] Bob Hasson with Danny Silk, *The Business of Honor: Restoring the Heart of Business* (Loving on Purpose, 2017), 29.

[2] Ibid, 81.

CHAPTER 8

Appreciation

"Appreciation is a wonderful thing: It makes
what is excellent in others belong to us as well."

—Voltaire

When I was in college, I worked at a beautifully restored colonial home that had been converted into a four-star hotel and restaurant. Even though my main job was to carry guests' bags to their rooms, my position was essentially a glorified gopher: I was supposed to do whatever anyone needed me to do. I reported to the innkeeper, Mr. Clarke, but I also had to do things for the front desk staff, the kitchen staff, and the bartender. Dave the bartender was a burly, gruff, middle-aged man with intense eyes and pursed lips; he was harsh with his words and quick to find fault—and I never seemed to do anything quite good enough for his taste. But I still had to work with Dave.

Other than the interactions with Dave, I enjoyed my time there. I enjoyed it there so much that I decided to apply to work there again the following summer. While filling out my application the next year,

I discovered that Mr. Clarke was no longer there—but Dave was. When I gave my application to the new innkeeper, he sought out Dave's advice about whether or not to hire me. To my surprise, Dave gave him an enthusiastic recommendation. Apparently I had met Dave's high standards, even though I thought I hadn't.

Even though Dave had a difficult demeanor, he did his job well and he expected the same of others. After learning of his surprise endorsement, I began to appreciate Dave's no-nonsense perspective. Even though he was hard, he was fair. He could provide an insightful assessment and not equivocate in his comments.

By changing your perception of your workplace, you will change you. You will enjoy yourself at work more because of how you choose to look at the situation.

You may have a boss who is as difficult to get along with as Dave, or more so. But it is important for you to look past that. Being able to appreciate your boss—no matter how difficult your situation may be—will help you improve your situation at work. In Chapter Two, one of the survey respondents said he wished his employees knew "How good they have it." That's why the Self-Leadership Question for this chapter is: *Do you appreciate your boss?*

Here are three things you can do to develop an appreciation for your boss.

1. Search for what you can appreciate

Even if you have a difficult boss, find something about your boss that you can appreciate (1 Timothy 2:1-2). I realize that you may say, "You don't know my boss!" Remember: that doesn't matter. This is not about your boss; this is about you.

Your time at work will be greatly improved if you can appreciate just one thing about your boss, like I did with Dave. Think through his or her abilities, demeanor, or comments. Find something, however small, that you can appreciate; then write it down, because you will need to remember it.

2. Express appreciation genuinely

Once you have found something to appreciate about your boss, think about it every time that you are together. Use it as a pair of "rose-colored glasses." Let that one thing you appreciate be the lens you look through to color how you see him or her. Eventually you will notice that your outlook about your boss will start to change.

Sometime when you are with your boss, go out of your way to say what you appreciate about him or her. Don't do it in a flattering way. Just say it like you mean it. If you really appreciate that one thing about your boss, you should be willing to say it—out loud.

Do not let your pride get in the way of appreciating your boss. Even if you have had difficulties with your boss, get past that. You will improve your relationship with your boss—and you will feel better about your work situation—if you verbally express your appreciation.

3. Cultivate a mindset of appreciation

Don't stop with appreciating your boss. Find something to appreciate about your annoying colleagues and your hectic workplace. Don't stop until you can find something that you can appreciate about everyone and everything at your workplace (1 Thessalonians 5:18; Ephesians 5:20).

When you are appreciating people, you are not "feeding their pride." Some people do not want to say what they appreciate about others for fear of making them prideful. That perspective is not helpful. People crave to be appreciated by others. You will bless them with your words of appreciation—and improve your relationship with them.

But ultimately this is not about the people at your workplace. This is about you. By changing your perception of your workplace, you will change *you*. You will enjoy yourself at work more because of how you *choose* to look at the situation.

As a result of finding things to appreciate about your colleagues, you will enjoy being around them more, like I found with Dave. People will be happier to work with you if you are happier with your work situation. You will find that your appreciation of others will have a boomerang effect: what you think about others will come back upon you as well.

Reflection Questions

1. What one thing can you appreciate about your boss?

2. How can you express what you appreciate about your boss to him or her?

3. What can you appreciate about others at your workplace? About the work itself?

CHAPTER 9

Respect

"There is no respect for others without humility in one's self."

—Henri Frederic Amiel

Many years ago I worked with a guy I'll call Brian. He was a go-getter. He was pro-active and responsible, but he had an unpredictable side. Once, Brian heard about a job he thought I would like, and he let me know about it. I applied for the position and got the job. Soon after, a job opening was announced in a different division in my workplace, and I thought it might be a fit for Brian. At the same time, I had this gnawing concern that it might not work out because of Brian's unpredictability. After debating back and forth with myself, I decided to tell Brian about the job—and recommend him for it—because he had told me about the job I currently had. I thought it was the right thing to do. But I still had that gnawing concern.

Not surprisingly, Brian got the job. Being the go-getter he was, he was not used to sitting and watching the extensive number of training videos required for the job. Every time I talked to Brian he seemed antsy. He wanted to do something. He knew he could contribute to the organization, but he didn't understand why his boss had him go

When you are content with the role that you have, you will enjoy your work more.

through so much training that he deemed unnecessary.

One day Brian's frustration hit a breaking point. He flew off the handle and said things to his boss that he shouldn't have said. As a result, he was fired on the spot. His actions in response appeared threatening, so he ended up being physically escorted off the premises.

Brian was a good worker, but his lack of respect for his boss got him fired. Perhaps you can sympathize or even relate with Brian. Perhaps you've had the same thing happen to you. Regardless of how you feel about what happened to Brian, he still needed to respect his boss.

Like Brian, you must be willing to respect your boss, even if you think your boss is wrong. One survey respondent in Chapter Two wished he could warn his employees, "don't forget I'm boss." Thus the Self-Leadership Question for this chapter is: *Do you respect your boss?*

Here are three ways to show your respect for your boss.

1. Respect the office
Even if you don't feel your boss deserves your respect, you still must respect the office that your boss holds. After all, he or she is the boss.

I realize that your boss may be annoying, insulting, or worse, but the fact is this person is in charge and you are not. You must respect that authority, whether good or bad (1 Peter 2:18). Your boss was placed in this position by God (Romans 13:1). By the very fact that your bosses have been placed in a position of authority, they deserve your respect (Romans 13:7). And if you resist those in authority over you, then you are bringing judgment upon yourself (Romans 13:2), just like what happened to Brian.

2. Respect decisions made

There may be times your boss will make decisions that you do not agree with. You may even think those decisions are ill-informed or stupid. But the fact is those decisions were made by someone in authority over you. And, like Brian, you have to respect those decisions (1 Thessalonians 5:12-13).

If you have an opportunity to give input into the decision making process, then by all means you should do so. But give your opinions respectfully. Then once those decisions are made, you should respect what has been decided.

3. Respect your role

You are at your place of work to execute the directives of your boss. If you can accept your boss's authority, it will go well with you. Remember: you serve at the pleasure of your boss, not the other way around.

When you are content with the role that you have, you will enjoy your work more (1 Timothy 6:6). You will do

> *Even if you don't feel your boss deserves your respect, you still must respect the office that your boss holds. After all, he or she is the boss.*

well to see yourself as a person under authority. You will find that you don't get as upset by decisions made if you are willing to accept that your job is to implement those decisions.

When you respect others, you respect yourself. When you respect those in authority over you, then it will go well with you (Romans 13:3-5). By respecting others, you are treating them the way you would want to be treated by them—and showing them how you would want them to treat you (Matthew 7:12).

Reflection Questions

1. How do you show respect to your boss?

2. In what ways do you respect the decisions made by your boss?

3. How have you shown respect for your role at work?

CHAPTER 10

Support

*"The purpose of human life is to serve,
and to show compassion and the will to help others."*

—Albert Schweitzer

Before his coronation as king, David spent many years as either Saul's court musician, as one of his military commanders, or as a hunted fugitive. Regardless of how Saul treated him, David referred to Saul as "king," "lord," and "the LORD's anointed."

One time Saul hunted for David in the wilderness of Engedi with 3,000 men. David and his men were hiding in a cave when Saul himself entered to relieve himself. David's men urged him to take his revenge. They told him that God gave him this opportunity to kill Saul. But David rebuked them and only cut off a corner of the king's garment. When Saul left the cave, David showed himself—and the corner of Saul's garment. David explained that his actions demonstrated that he supported the king, even though the king was against him (1 Samuel 24).

Even if you think your boss is out to get you, your relationship with your boss is not as bad as it was for David. But even though

If you support your boss, you will find that your influence with your boss will grow.

Saul wanted David dead, David still honored the king with his support—and you should honor your boss with your support. In Chapter Two, we saw that one boss wanted his employees to know that "I'm working hard for them." Turning that comment around, the Self-Leadership Question in this chapter is: *Do you support your boss?*

In Scripture, John rebuked Diotrephes for his lack of support (3 John 9-10). Looking at what Diotrephes *didn't* do to support John, here are three things you *should* do to support your boss.

1. Support your boss with your words
John mentioned that Diotrephes was "talking wicked nonsense against us" (3 John 10). His words no doubt caused problems for John because he took the time to mention it to Gaius in his letter. John also suggested that Diotrephes' actions actually "imitate evil" (3 John 11). The things you say to others in the workplace will either "imitate evil" or "imitate good." You get to choose whether your words will be supportive or unsupportive.

Now, if your boss is doing illegal things, then by all means you should report that to the appropriate authorities. However, if you merely don't like what your boss is doing, then do not badmouth him or her. Your boss is accountable to God for his or her words. And you are accountable to God for yours.

2. Support your boss with your actions
John said that Diotrephes "refuses to welcome the brothers" who came to Gaius from another place (3 John 10). Not only did Diotrephes speak against John, he avoided helping those who John commended

to Gaius. As a result, Gaius did not receive the support he ought to have had from Diotrephes.

Evaluate your boss's strengths and weaknesses. How can you enhance his or her strengths? How can you fill in for his or her weaknesses? If you were the boss, what kind of support would you need in your position? Be the kind of support to your boss that you would want to have. If you support your boss, you will find that your influence with your boss will grow.

You can always choose to leave your place of employment. However, if you choose to stay, you should actively support your boss. Like Saul, your boss is accountable to God for his or her actions, just as you are accountable for yours.

3. Help others support the boss with their actions

John explained that Diotrephes "stops those who want to [welcome the brothers] and puts them out of the church" (3 John 10). Diotrephes was not content to refuse to welcome the brothers; he didn't want anyone else to welcome them and actively worked against them.

Like David, be willing to encourage others to support your boss. He or she is in authority over you, and you should be willing to acknowledge that authority. After all, you chose to work there. By staying there, you are choosing to remain under that authority.

By supporting your boss, you are supporting an authority who God has placed in that position. And your support of that authority will be met with God's approval (Romans 13:3).

Reflection Questions

1.   How much do you support your boss with your words?

2.   How much do you support your boss with your actions?

3.   How much do you help others support your boss?

CHAPTER 11

Paradigm Shift #2
Open

"Honest communication is built on truth and integrity and upon respect of the one for the other."

—Benjamin E. Mays

Many years ago I started a new job near the end of the calendar year. After being on the job for just weeks, an issue arose during the holidays that I thought my boss should be aware of. I didn't want to hide the situation from him, but neither did I want to bother my boss while he was on vacation with his family. Determining that this issue could not wait, I decided it was best to call him. Although he seemed surprised that I disturbed his time away from the office, he thanked me for the information.

Over the following months, I continued to cultivate an open policy with my boss. I brought forward issues that he needed to be aware of. I gave my boss all the facts and didn't sugarcoat the situation. I provided him sufficient information and recommendations to make good management decisions. And in less than two years' time, my boss promoted me to the highest position in the office, second only to himself.

Like my boss, your boss is not a mind reader. He or she doesn't know everything you know unless you share the information. Your boss likely doesn't know as much about the details of your job as you do, so provide an opportunity for a free-flow of information. That opportunity for dialogue could end up getting you promoted—just like it happened to me.

Even if you and your boss have not seen eye to eye, resolve to pursue open communication from now on. Be conscious of the words that you use in your conversations. When you share information, don't say dishonoring or disrespectful things that will close off communication.

Open communication is essential in your workplace, and you should do all you can encourage it. As I said in my first book, *Dear Boss: What Your Employees Wish You Knew*, "Look at information like water: It stagnates when it stays in one place. Help the information flow in your company, and do not let it stagnate with you."[1]

Your openness can help transform your workplace, if you are willing to be part of the solution,

> *Look at information like water: It stagnates when it stays in one place. Help the information flow in your company, and do not let it stagnate with you.*

and not part of the problems. In this section, we will explore what Open looks like. In each chapter about Open, I will pose a Self-Leadership question based on a survey response in a preceding chapter. In the next three chapters, we will explore the following three topics.

1. Straightforwardness
Communicate job-related problems so your boss can help you solve them. It is also important to report issues in a timely manner so that they can be addressed quickly.

2. Integrity
Be honest all the time. Exhibit integrity in everything you do. Always stay above reproach. Otherwise, it may well come back to bite you.

3. Transparency
Learn to communicate transparently and effectively with your boss. It is important to allow for information to flow freely to management without any hidden agendas.

I am hopeful that these chapters will help you see how being open with your boss will benefit you, your boss, and the organization as a whole.

Reflection Questions

1. How straightforward have you been with your boss up to this point?

2. How honest have you been with your boss up to this point?

3. How transparent have you been with your boss up to this point?

Notes
_____

1   Robert McFarland, *Dear Boss: What Your Employees Wish You Knew* (Pasadena: Best Seller Publishing, 2017), 174.

CHAPTER 12

Straightforwardness

"I find that really good leaders ... want the truth.
And you do them a service, and yourself a service,
by just being honest and straightforward."

—Daniel Pink

The New Testament paints a picture of the Apostle Paul as a passionate evangelist who was not afraid to say hard things. As was his typical manner, Paul was straightforward in his second letter to the Corinthians: "For I fear that perhaps when I come I may find you not as I wish, and that you may find me not as you wish—that perhaps there may be quarreling, jealousy, anger, hostility, slander, gossip, conceit, and disorder" (1 Corinthians 12:20).

Paul wrote directly to his audience because he was not concerned about offending sensibilities. He knew that truth was at stake, so he spoke plainly, not avoiding difficult subjects. At the same time, Paul had earned the right to be heard. He had developed a relationship with the people who heard his Good News, so they were willing to also hear his rebukes. As he prepared to visit the Corinthians, he showed his care for them in his plainspoken style.

> Here for the third time I am ready to come to you. And I will not be a burden, for I seek not what is yours but you. For children are not obligated to save up for their parents, but parents for their children. I will most gladly spend and be spent for your souls. ...

> Your restoration is what we pray for. For this reason I write these things while I am away from you, that when I come I may not have to be severe in my use of the authority that the Lord has given me *for building up* and *not for tearing down*. (2 Corinthians 12:14-15a, 13:9b-10)

Paul made it clear that he wanted to build up the Corinthians. He was straightforward with the Corinthians not for the sake of being straightforward, but because he cared for their wellbeing. As a result, his genuine concern for them allowed them to receive the hard things that he said.

In your relationship with your boss, there may be times when you will need to say hard things that you may not want to say, but you need to be willing to say them. You may need to report a problem that you need help solving. There may be personnel concerns that will become bigger problems if left on their own. While you may not want to have to bring your boss into the issue, it could become worse if not addressed in a timely manner. As Rick Whitted shares in *Outgrow Your Space at Work*,

> failing to be honest with management about your concerns can turn an isolated issue into everybody's problem. ... Your boss wants and needs to know about conflicts within their team. Bringing issues or potential problems to their attention is an opportunity to demonstrate your leadership and professional maturity. I've seen many employees keep quiet until they are absolutely miserable. This is a mistake, because problems never age well.[1]

No one wants to be the bearer of bad news. People don't like to have direct and difficult conversations. But you show genuine concern for your boss and your workplace when you are willing to share that bad news.

Proverbs 27:6 says "Faithful are the wounds of a friend." If you care enough about your work situation to help improve it, then everybody wins. But you have to be willing to take the first step to say hard things. At the same time, you want to make sure that what you say will be received. Proverbs 15:1 says "A soft answer turns away wrath, but a harsh word stirs up anger." Be wise about how you say what you say. Otherwise, you may damage your relationship with your boss. Then nobody wins.

> *If you care enough about your work situation to help improve it, then everybody wins.*

Be strong, but be smart. Be willing to say what must be said in a way that your boss would welcome you to share it again, if you had to. In Chapter Three one of the bosses wanted his employees to know "How to say what they need." In response, this chapter's Self-Leadership Question is: *Can you say what needs to be said in a straightforward but caring way?*

Here are three reasons why you should approach saying hard things in a straightforward way.

1. Saying hard things is helpful

The first half of Proverbs 13:24 equates saying hard things with caring. If you won't say hard things, then you're saying you don't care.

You might not want to say hard things to your boss because you're concerned about how your boss will respond. Be willing to care about your boss enough to say the hard things. And that will make it easier for you to tell your boss what needs to be said.

2. Be wise in saying hard things

You can help everyone at your workplace by sharing information with your boss that will make him or her better. But you may need to get permission to say it first. You can ask your boss, "If I knew something that would help you do your job better, would you want me to tell you?" If your boss says yes, then you have permission to say whatever you need to say. If you genuinely want to help your boss, then your genuine concern will show through.

Don't put off saying what needs to be said. It won't do you any good.

3. Be diligent to say hard things

Don't put off saying what needs to be said. It won't do you any good. And it certainly won't help your boss. If it needs to be said, it's best to get it out in the open. You might as well get it over with so you can move forward. You don't want to prolong the inevitable for either of you.

You can improve your workplace by saying what needs to be said—but like Paul, you have to be brave enough to say it.

Reflection Questions

1. Have you avoided saying hard things in the past? How did that go?

2. Have you put off saying hard things until it was too late? What happened as a result?

3. How could you say hard things in a way that your boss would receive it?

Notes

[1] Rick Whitted, *Outgrow Your Space at Work: How to Thrive at Work and Build a Successful Career* (Grand Rapids: Revell, 2016), 191.

CHAPTER 13

Integrity

"With integrity, you have nothing to fear,
since you have nothing to hide."

—Zig Ziglar

Before I started Transformational Impact LLC, I worked with my friend Ben Case. Ben is reputedly one of the best major gift fundraisers in the world, having helped nonprofits raise more than $4.8 billion in his 41 years in fundraising and nonprofit management. Ben has also been a hallmark of honesty and integrity as long as I have known him. He tells a powerful story to explain the importance of integrity.

> I was in a meeting with my wife, Angela, and Robert McFarland, at the time a consultant with our company. ... I was deeply resisting something Angela insisted I do. Angela thought that, as a business owner, I was required by law to do this. Our lawyer acknowledged there were "gray areas" as to the applicability of the law to our work. Give me "gray areas" and I will run with it forever. I did not want to do what Angela was telling me to do! Then Robert, who had been observing the discussion and my strong resistance,

simply asked, "Ben, when are you going to have integrity— some of the time or all of the time?"

Live with integrity. In the walk of life, you will always be glad you did. Integrity means all the time. ...

I did follow my wife's advice, and am glad I did.[1]

As Ben said, integrity means all the time. It is possible to be honest in one situation but not in another, but you can't choose to have integrity one day and not the next. It's all or nothing. Either you have integrity or you don't.

In his book *The Deeper Life*, Daniel Henderson gives a good definition of integrity: "Integrity is a life where all the pieces fit together."[2] If you have integrity, then your life is integrated. You are not one way with some people and another way with other people. You are the same person all the time.

> *You can't choose to have integrity one day and not the next. It's all or nothing. Either you have integrity or you don't.*

Henderson also explains what integrity is not: "compartmentalization is the opposite of integrity."[3] If you have to keep one part of your life separate from the rest of your life, you lead a compartmentalized life. If your Sunday is separate from your Monday through Saturday, you do not have an integrated life.

Integrity is about being honest with yourself: you know the real truth about the person you see in the mirror. You may be able to fool other people, but you can't fool yourself. You have to be with yourself all the time, and you know if you are trustworthy.

You need to be *trustworthy* all the time if you want to be *trusted* all the time. It's crucial to have a track record of trustworthiness in order for your boss to want to trust you. In Chapter Three, one of the bosses from the survey wanted his employees to know "That I can tell when they are lying." In light of that comment, the Self-Leadership Question for this chapter is: *Can you be counted on to exhibit integrity all the time?*

> *You need to be trustworthy all the time if you want to be trusted all the time.*

Here are three things to keep in mind to help you exhibit integrity.

1. Know yourself

The first step to have integrity is to know who you should be. If you know who you should be, then you can catch yourself when you're not.

Do you find yourself in situations where you compromise your integrity? Do you feel you have to be someone in certain situations you don't want to be? If so, why is that? And what does that tell you about yourself? When you find yourself in those situations, remind yourself who you should be, so you can avoid being who you shouldn't be.

2. Talk straight

Mark Twain supposedly said, "Always tell the truth. Then you don't have to remember what you said." While it may seem funny, that quip contains a lot of truth. If you always tell the truth, then you don't have to keep track of what you said to each person. Your story is always the same.

Be willing to speak the truth in all situations at work. If your boss catches you telling even one lie, then your trustworthiness can be permanently compromised. But if you are willing to say the truth—even when you have to say hard things—then you will consistently be believed.

> *Think through how you want to be remembered. Then be that way all the time.*

3. Act right

James 1:8 says that a double-minded man is unstable in all his ways. The Greek word for *double-minded* means "two-spirited," or you could even say it means "two-faced." If you are trying to act like two different people, then you will sacrifice your integrity and be unstable in all your ways.

Think through how you want to be remembered. Then be that way all the time.

As Ben explained, if you want to be known as a person of integrity, then you will have to be that person of integrity all the time.

Reflection Questions

1.   How well do you know yourself?

2.   How often do you talk straight?

3.   How often are you the person you want to be?

Notes

[1]   Benjamin R. Case, "When Are You Going to Have Integrity—Some of the Time or All of the Time? Integrity Means All the Time." http://www.robertmcfarland. net/integrity-means-all-the-time/, accessed June 20, 2018.

[2]   Daniel Henderson, *The Deeper Life: Satisfying the 8 Vital Longings of the Soul* (Bloomington, MN: Bethany House Publishers, 2014), 20.

[3]   Ibid, 19.

CHAPTER 14

Transparency

"The single most important ingredient in the recipe for success is transparency because transparency builds trust."

—Denise Morrison

Several years ago, I hired a guy I'll call Ed. He came highly recommended by a good friend of mine. Ed spoke well, he represented himself well, and he seemed like an all-around good guy. He seemed like he had the abilities to do the job well. Or so I thought.

Not long into the job I realized that this arrangement was not working out. He was not able to do the work, and he was not able to meet deadlines. But what frustrated me most was that he did not tell me about the difficulties he was experiencing. I found out things were not going well when it was almost too late to do anything about the situation.

When I shared my concerns with him, he said he had everything under control. That eroded his credibility with me even further. At his 90-day review, I decided that I had to let him go. While his job performance was lacking, I fired him primarily because of his lack of transparency.

Transparency is not an easy thing to come by because it is not typically practiced in the business world, or in personal living. In my first book, *Dear Boss: What Your Employees Wish You Knew*, I described our society's lack of transparency.

> Most communication scenarios are designed to conceal information rather than disclose it. When a couple is dating, most of their time together seems to be designed to position themselves in the best light, rather than to share information transparently with someone who may become their future spouse. When an applicant comes in for a job interview, he reveals only the amount of information that will help him secure the job—especially if the information he conceals would show he and the company would be a bad fit for each other. When unions and management are in contract negotiations, both sides try to get the most out of the situation, and they will reveal only what they perceive will benefit their side. As a result, transparency is not the norm.[1]

Transparency is different from simply telling the truth. Someone can tell the truth but not really give the whole truth. Stephen M. R. Covey in *The Speed of Trust* explains how people can tell the truth and yet still deceive.

> Most people don't flat-out lie—at least not blatantly. Instead they engage in the *counterfeit* behaviors ... such as beating around the bush, withholding information, double-talk (speaking with a "forked tongue"), flattery, positioning, posturing, and the granddaddy of them all: "spinning" communication in order to manipulate the thoughts, feelings, or actions of others. Another dangerous counterfeit is "technically" telling the truth but leaving a false impression. This is mincing words and legally splitting hairs. All these behaviors invariably diminish trust.[2]

A physical object that is transparent is see-through. You can literally see right through it. If you are being transparent, people can see right through you. You are not trying to hide anything. If a conversation is transparent, then information—like light—is able to move freely between sides, and neither party is left in the dark. If you are transparent with your boss, then your boss will know that you are fully open. You are sharing all there is to share. Transparency provides the occasion for fully disclosing information and being fully trusted.

> *If a conversation is transparent, then information— like light—is able to move freely between sides, and neither party is left in the dark.*

Transparency is key to good communication and having real dialogue. If you are not being transparent, you and your boss can be exchanging words but not really communicating. In *Outgrow Your Space at Work*, Rick Whitted explains that issues you have with your boss may not be your boss's fault. "Sometimes there are managers who do a lousy job of engaging their employees and creating an environment of ownership, creativity, and teamwork. However, it's just as common for employees not to proactively engage their managers because of their personal assumptions about them. This is usually driven by personality differences."[3]

Even if you don't particularly like to be around your boss, taking the initiative to talk with your boss may yield surprising results. Communicating openly can change the relationship with your boss —and *you* can be the one to initiate that change. In Chapter Three, one of the bosses from the survey wanted his employees to know "how to communicate effectively." As a result, this chapter's Self-Leadership Question is: *Are you transparent with your boss?*

Here are three ways to improve how you share information with your boss.

1. Share information quickly

Unlike Ed, be quick to share information with your boss. Do not let too much time go by before you share any updates. Be sure to tell your boss quickly if

- new developments arise in a volatile situation,
- changes occur that affect safety for employees, or
- the media show up to ask you any questions.

These are all situations where your boss will want to know sooner rather than later, and these are all scenarios where you don't want all the attention focused on you.

2. Share information freely

Do not try to hide information from your boss like Ed did. If productivity slips, if someone gets injured, or if someone is violating proper procedure, you should share that information with your boss. While you may not want to be the bearer of bad news, it's better to share these items while something can be done to fix the situation, rather than when it's too late.

If you are not being transparent, you and your boss can be exchanging words but not really communicating.

Proactively ask your boss if there is a particular way to handle sensitive situations before they arise. That way it won't be as awkward for you to share sensitive information. You can also ask your boss to create a suggestion box, where you can anonymously pass along information as necessary. That way everyone can save face, and you can look out for the best interests of the organization.

3. Share information effectively

Try to communicate as much information as you can in the fewest words possible. That way you will be able to keep your boss's attention, while still saying what needs to be said.

If you get nervous when you have to talk with your boss in person, write down what you want to say in advance and then read it over. That will help you collect your thoughts and be more efficient with your boss's time. You can also ask someone to read what you've written to make sure it makes sense before you share it with your boss. If it doesn't make sense, go back and rewrite it so that it is clear. Then you'll be ready to share it with your boss.

By making the effort to share information quickly, freely, and effectively, you will enhance your working relationship with your boss.

By making the effort to share information quickly, freely, and effectively, you will enhance your working relationship with your boss. Your openness and transparency will help you create an environment where your boss will trust you more.

Reflection Questions

1. When have you not shared information in a timely manner? What did you learn from that?

2. When have you seen information deliberately hidden from the boss? What happened?

3. In what ways can you share information more effectively with your boss?

Notes

1. Robert McFarland, *Dear Boss: What Your Employees Wish You Knew* (Pasadena: Best Seller Publishing, 2017), 154.

2. Stephen M. R. Covey, *The Speed of Trust: The One Thing That Changes Everything* (New York: Free Press, 2006), 138-139.

3. Rick Whitted, *Outgrow Your Space at Work: How to Thrive at Work and Build a Successful Career* (Grand Rapids: Revell, 2016), 187.

CHAPTER 15

Paradigm Shift #3
Perceptive

"To be a champion, I think you have to see the big picture."

—Summer Sanders

In *Business for the Common Good*, Kenman Wong and Scott Rae tell a great story about the power of seeing the big picture.

> As Bill Pollard, former CEO of ServiceMaster, says, "People want to contribute to a cause, not just earn a living." ...
>
> Pollard tells the story of Shirley, one of the housekeepers for their hospital janitorial services division. To an outsider her position might look like a dead-end job with no purpose other than an economic transaction. But at ServiceMaster these positions have significance. ...
>
> > Shirley sees her work as extending to the welfare of the patient and as an integral part of a team that helps sick people get well. She has a cause that involves the health and welfare of others. When

Shirley first started, no doubt she was merely looking for just a job. But she brought to her work an unlocked potential and a desire to accomplish something significant. As I talked with Shirley about her job, she said, "If we don't clean with a quality effort, we can't keep the doctors and nurses in business. We can't serve the patients. *This place would be closed if we didn't have housekeeping.*" ...

Shirley had a clear sense of purpose for her work, which kept her coming back to work motivated for many years.[1]

You can choose to see that your job is meaningless, or you can decide—as Shirley did—to believe that your job has purpose and is part of accomplishing a bigger picture. It's your choice. By seeing that your job is part of something bigger, you will catch sight of how the pieces fit together.

After I guest lectured to MBA students at a local university about my first book, *Dear Boss: What Your Employees Wish You Knew*, one of the students asked me a question about alignment. She wanted to understand the role of a leader in creating company culture. I told her one of the most important things a leader can do to create culture: connect long-term goals to short-term actions. Leaders can do that best by sharing the big picture. Focusing on the big picture—one day at a time, one conversation at a time—will help a leader build the culture of an organization.

> *By seeing that your job is part of something bigger, you will catch sight of how the pieces fit together.*

Along those same lines, it is just as important for all employees—not just leaders—to see the big picture. Everyone must be able to understand and embrace that vision. It will help direct their individual short-term actions to achieve corporate long-term goals.

The little actions you do every day are important to accomplishing a bigger goal. No job is exciting all the time. There are times that every job will have its drudgery. It's your choice whether you will see your efforts affecting only your job, or if you will see your efforts contributing to the big picture.

> *It is just as important for all employees— not just leaders—to see the big picture.*

Everyone's job is important. It doesn't matter how seemingly insignificant you think your job may be, it is important to the overall purpose of the organization. Every job interrelates with what the company ultimately does. The piece that you do is important to everyone else. But you have to see and believe that—just like Shirley did.

In this section, we will explore what Perceptive looks like. For each chapter about Perceptive, I will pose a Self-Leadership question based on a comment made by a survey respondent. Over the next three chapters, we will explore the following three topics.

1. Perspective
Understand that your boss is human: If you were in his or her shoes, you might likely respond similarly. Try to see the overall picture as well as understand how your job fits into the overall organization.

2. Procedure
Realize that there are certain procedures you must follow, whether it is for safety or just because your boss wants it done that way. There are benefits for doing it the right way and consequences for doing it the wrong way.

3. Representation

Whether you are at work or not, you are always representing the company—even if you do not interface directly with customers. As a result, it is important to maintain a positive attitude about the company—particularly if you are with customers.

After reading these chapters, I hope you, like Shirley, will see how you can have more influence in improving your company—as well as your own career.

Reflection Questions

1. What perspective do you have of the role you play in the company you work for?

2. What procedures affect what you do?

3. To what degree do you represent your company—on and off the job?

Notes

[1] Kenman L. Wong and Scott B. Rae, *Business for the Common Good: A Christian Vision for the Marketplace* (Madison, WI: InterVarsity Press, 2011), 208-209.

CHAPTER 16

Perspective

"The only thing you sometimes have control over is perspective."

—Chris Pine

At one place I worked, I facilitated the onboarding process for new hires from around the country. I guided them through their orientation as well as their introduction to their initial corporate training. During this time, these new hires were exposed to the depth of the organization. They discovered for the first time all the services their employer provided to clients. Even though it might have felt overwhelming, they got a full picture of the capabilities of their new employer. By learning of all the ways they could be a part of serving their clients, they gained a newfound perspective.

In the sixth chapter of 2 Kings, the Scripture shows how important perspective is. After the prophet Elisha had repeatedly warned the king of Israel of the Syrian king's battle plans, one night the infuriated king of Syria travelled to the city where Elisha was in order to capture him. The next morning, Elisha's servant woke up to see this vast army surrounding the city. Consequently, the servant was terrified.

And the servant said, "Alas, my master! What shall we do?" He said, "Do not be afraid, for those who are with us are more than those who are with them." Then Elisha prayed and said, "O Lord, please open his eyes that he may see." So the LORD opened the eyes of the young man, and he saw, and behold, the mountain was full of horses and chariots of fire all around Elisha. (2 Kings 6:15b-17)

Elisha had a perspective that his servant did not have. Only when his servant looked at the situation the same way Elisha did was he able to see what Elisha could see. It is easy to assume that your perspective is the only one. But your perspective may not be accurate. There may be some information that you are not aware of, like Elisha's servant discovered. What you don't know can affect how you see the situation. Therefore, it is important for you to be willing to look beyond your own perspective.

Take time to reflect before you pass judgment on your boss or your workplace. Realize that there may be more to the situation than meets your eye. John Maxwell says it well in *How Successful People Think*:

> When you reflect, you are able to put an experience into perspective. You are able to evaluate its timing. And you are able to gain a new appreciation for things that before went unnoticed. ... That's the kind of perspective that comes with reflection. ...
>
> When you engage in reflective thinking, you can put ideas and experiences into a more accurate context. ... Without reflection, it can be very difficult to see that big picture.[1]

Stepping back to see the big picture helps you understand how everything at your workplace fits together. This perspective can help you realize there may be more going on that you were initially aware of, as the new hires discovered at their orientation. In Chapter

Four, one of the respondents to the survey said that he wished his employees knew "How their job fits into the overall organization." Accordingly, the Self-Leadership Question for this chapter is: *Are you willing to see yourself from your boss's perspective?*

Here are three ways you can look at your role at your workplace to gain a new perspective.

1. See yourself through your boss's eyes

You may be aware that your actions impact your boss, but so do your thoughts. Your self-perception—the way that you perceive yourself—affects your relationship with your boss. If you are willing to look at yourself objectively, then you have the opportunity to enhance not only your relationship with your boss, but also the prospects for your career. However, if you think that your perspective cannot be wrong, then you may be in for some rude awakenings throughout your career.

It is important to be willing to admit that you may not always be right. You may not have a correct assessment of the situation. Until you can see your situation from an unbiased vantage point, you may not have an accurate picture of what's going on.

Taking your boss's perspective requires that you are able to get out of your own way. By honestly assessing how your boss perceives you, you can be aware of the effect your actions have on your boss.

Having the self-awareness to perceive accurately how you impact your boss will serve you well. But it

> *Until you can see your situation from an unbiased vantage point, you may not have an accurate picture of what's going on.*

takes humility to step back and force yourself to think through what your boss may want you to know about yourself.

2. Look at yourself from the team's vantage point

Look at how your job impacts the rest of your team. Be aware of your performance on the job and how other people look at the work you do.

Your team may not tell you how your performance impacts them, so you may have to look for body language clues. Do they try to leave before you come in the room? Do they not make eye contact with you? If so, there may be something that needs to be resolved with your team.

If you have had difficulty getting along with your team, then take responsibility for your part and apologize for it. Apologizing for past problems will not make you lose credibility; on the contrary, it will actually put you in a better stead with your team. They already know how you have contributed to the problems. Denying that there was ever a problem is not the way to make the problems better. Acknowledging your part in what has happened in the past will allow you to clear the air and work together better in the future.

What you don't know can affect how you see the situation. Therefore, it is important for you to be willing to look beyond your own perspective.

3. View your role as part of the whole

Try to see how your job fits into the big picture, as the new hires did. Look at how your work impacts the rest of the organization. Think through the importance of your work. Understand why your work matters to the rest of the team. Then do your work to the best of your ability.

Realize that there are many working parts at your organization. Believe that what you do matters, and resolve to do it the best you can. Choose to benefit the organization through how you do your work.

Do not be discouraged if your work seems small in the big picture. Remember that all work has meaning and significance, and that includes *your* work and how you do it.

Reflection Questions

1. How does your boss see you? Do you think you make your boss's life easier or more difficult?

2. How does your team see you? Do you come through for your team or do you leave them hanging?

3. How can you do your work to be a benefit to everyone at your workplace?

Notes
_____

[1] John C. Maxwell, *How Successful People Think: Change Your Thinking, Change Your Life* (New York: Center Street, 2009), 72-74.

CHAPTER 17

Procedure

"If you can't describe what you are doing as a process,
you don't know what you are doing."

—W. Edwards Deming

When King David wanted to bring the ark of God from Kiriath-jearim to his palace in Jerusalem, he consulted with the leaders of the tribes of Israel. David sought to verify that the leaders thought it was a good idea to bring the ark back into regular use since the ark had not been part of their religious observances under his predecessor, King Saul. While all the leaders supported his idea, David neglected to consult one key group: the Levites. The Levites were the ones God had specifically tasked to take care of the ark. They were the ones who cared for it for generations. But it had been many years since the ark had occupied a central place in their culture, and David had forgotten the important role the Levites played in dealing with the ark.

A big celebration had been put into place to observe moving the ark to Jerusalem. Two brothers, Uzzah and Ahio, were driving the cart which carried the ark. Everyone was celebrating with all kinds of musical instruments. However, at one point, the oxen stumbled and Uzzah touched the ark to steady it, and God struck him dead on the spot. David was angry at God because he killed Uzzah on this festive occasion, and he wondered how he could ever take the ark back to Jerusalem with him.

Three months later David realized his mistake: "no one but the Levites may carry the ark of God, for the LORD had chosen them

Fighting against the rules will not help you.

to carry the ark of the LORD and to minister to him forever." David assembled all the leaders of the Levites and told them the seriousness of their task: "Because you did not carry it the first time, the LORD our God broke out against us, because we did not seek him according to the rule" (1 Chronicles 13:1-13; 15:2, 13). God had instituted a specific procedure for carrying the ark. It didn't matter that the people didn't remember it. God's rule was still in effect.

In your workplace, there may be certain ways of doing things that must be observed. But you may not always be aware of what they are. Or you may dislike these procedures. You might even think some of these procedures are unnecessary. But they have been put into place for a reason.

Fighting against the rules will not help you. Digging below the surface of the rules can help you figure out why they are in place to begin with. In Chapter Four, one of the bosses who responded to the survey said she wished her employees knew that "[It's] easier to do it the right way than to take short cuts doing it the wrong way." As a result, the Self-Leadership Question in this chapter is: *Are you aware of the policies and procedures you should follow at your workplace?*

Here are the ABC's of learning the procedures that are in effect in your workplace.

1. Awareness

Become a student of the policies and procedures at your workplace. Some of these rules may have been put in place for legal or safety reasons. But some procedures may be in place only because your boss prefers it to be done that way.

Be aware that there may be procedures at your workplace that are not written down. It is valuable for you to be aware of how your organization always does things—and never does things. Even if you don't agree with these procedures, be a student of the way things are done at your workplace. It is important to know how it is supposed to be done—whether or not you like it.

2. Benefits

Find out the benefits of following the policies and procedures. As David discovered, the rules can be there to keep you out of trouble or out of harm. Both are good reasons to observe standard procedure.

You might find that observing these procedures gets you on the good side of your boss, if you do it the way that he or she likes. If there is nothing immoral, illegal, or unethical with doing it his or her specified way—and it benefits you to do it that way—then you might as well start doing it that way.

3. Consequences

Know the consequences of not adhering to the policies and procedures. Shortcuts that could hurt someone are not really shortcuts. Also, doing it the right way the first time may save you a lot of time in the long run. You don't want to have to redo work you thought you had completed.

In addition, you can run the risk of raising the ire of your boss if you do not follow the specified procedures. Count the cost of crossing that line. Ask yourself if the consequences will be worth it. Even if you don't agree with the rules, it may be best to abide by them.

Make the effort to be fully informed of the rules at your workplace. Then determine the benefits and consequences of following both the written and unwritten rules. Like David, you may find that the required procedures are more important than you initially realized.

Reflection Questions

1. What policies and procedures, whether written or unwritten, are you aware of at your workplace?

2. What are the benefits of following these policies and procedures?

3. What are the consequences of not following them?

CHAPTER 18

Representation

"People may hear your words, but they feel your attitude."
—John C. Maxwell

Many years ago I worked for a guy I'll call Greg. Working with Greg was awkward. He badmouthed his boss in the office, but in public he spoke favorably about him. To outsiders, he seemed like a good team player, but those of us who worked for him knew otherwise.

Greg got a promotion that gave him even greater autonomy. His role involved more travel and he had more opportunities to represent his boss and the organization. While he was competent at what he did, he still did not have a positive opinion of his boss.

One day, Greg's opinions caught up to him. He was dismissed for disloyalty to his boss and to the organization. Despite getting caught, he did not express remorse over how he handled the situation. Instead he blamed his boss.

When Greg said disparaging things about his boss, it was less a statement about his boss and more a statement about himself. While he represented his boss he also represented himself, and what he said about his boss within the office reflected poorly on himself.

When you represent your boss, you also represent yourself. How you conduct yourself representing your employer says a lot about you. Perhaps you complain about your employer to others so that they will join you in complaining about their employers. At best, it drags you down to a lower level. At worst, it poisons your relationship with other people and damages your prospects at getting employed elsewhere.

> *Whether you deal directly with customers or not, you represent your employer to people in your sphere of influence.*

Rick Whitted gives sage advice in his book *Outgrow Your Space at Work*. "Changing your attitude toward your current job, the people around you, and your current employer is the most decisive way to outgrow your space at work and build and thrive in a career that lasts."[1] But it is up to you whether you change your attitude and choose to represent yourself and your employer in a way that honors both you and your company. No one can improve your attitude for you. As I quoted Chuck Swindoll in Chapter One, you have to be the one who will decide to change your attitude.

Whether you deal directly with customers or not, you represent your employer to people in your sphere of influence. In Chapter Four, one boss wanted her employees to know that "They are the face of the company and our 1st impression to our customers." Along those lines, the Self-Leadership Question for this chapter is: *Do you represent your employer well on and off the job?*

Here are three areas in which you should monitor your attitude to represent yourself and your employer well.

1. Beliefs about your boss

Be watchful about how you feel about your employer because it says a lot about *you*. The more you complain about your employer, the more people will think that the issue is with you and not your employer.

No prospective employer wants to hire a Greg who badmouths his current or previous employer. Your future employers will be able to determine what you will think of them based on what you say about your current and previous bosses.

Be watchful about how you feel about your employer because it says a lot about you.

Consider what you think and say about your employer—even when you're not on the job. You never know who may be listening. If a potential employer hears you complain about your current employer outside of an interview, it's very possible that you won't get the opportunity to interview with them.

2. Beliefs about your work

People do their work based on what they believe about their work. More often than not, when I call Customer Service, I end up talking to someone who doesn't want to talk with me. One time the person who answered the phone gave a long introductory statement, but I couldn't understand a word of it. He said the greeting so fast that it was unintelligible to me. Later that day, I had to call the same company, and I got the same person on the other end of the phone. Again, he said the greeting so fast that I barely caught a few words of it. Having heard this hurried greeting a second time, I thought to myself, "This business should not have their people say this long introduction at the start of every phone call. It makes the company sound ridiculous." But then I realized the person answering the phone had a responsibility in this situation as well. He could choose to rush through saying this introduction and sound ridiculous, or he could choose to slow down and say it in a way that represented both himself the company well. It depends on what he believes about his work.

You may say, "But you don't know what my job is like!" And you're right; I probably don't know what your job is like. However, that doesn't matter. If you think what you have to do at your job is beneath you, it will affect how you do your job. How you do your job now will also affect what kind of employment prospects you have in the future. It behooves you to think highly of the work that you do now. Do it well, so you can improve your future employment prospects.

3. Beliefs about the people you interact with
Whether or not you work directly with customers, you will likely have to deal with colleagues, suppliers, or vendors. If you complain about the people who work with you, you may find that they think the same thing about you. If there is a "someone" that you complain about, then you could be the "someone" that they complain about.

People do their work based on what they believe about their work.

Bad feelings can boomerang. You reap what you sow (Galatians 6:7).

When you have *contact* with people, you may have *conflict* with people. However, you can choose to look differently at the people around you. You don't have to respond to people the way that you see others respond to you (Colossians 3:13).

You will enjoy your time at work more if you choose to look at the people around you in the way that they *could be*, not necessarily the way they *are*—because that is the way you would want others to look at you if the situation were reversed (Matthew 7:12).

Don't be like Greg. Instead, resolve to represent yourself and your employer in a way that will put both of you in the best light. That will enable you to rise above whatever problems you have to deal with at the workplace. And you will see your influence increase.

Reflection Questions

1. What do you believe about your employer? Do you complain about your boss?

2. What do you believe about your work? And what does that say about you?

3. What do you believe about the people you work with? Would you want them to believe that about you?

Notes

[1] Rick Whitted, *Outgrow Your Space at Work: How to Thrive at Work and Build a Successful Career* (Grand Rapids: Revell, 2016), 195.

CHAPTER 19

Paradigm Shift #4
Engaged

*"Teamwork requires some sacrifice upfront;
people who work as a team have to put the collective
needs of the group ahead of their individual interests."*

—Patrick Lencioni

A long time ago, I worked for a small public policy organization on Capitol Hill. Once, my boss helped bring sitting members of the Russian Duma to the United States to have public talks with their counterparts in the U.S. Congress. As Director of Media Relations, my task was to organize that forum and to get it covered in the national press. I was willing to take on the task, but we were a small nonprofit, and I had a staff of none.

Given assurances that the Deputies (or Duma members) would be in the United States on a specific day, I secured commitments from members of the U.S. Senate Foreign Relations Committee and the House Foreign Affairs Committee to participate. I retained translation services for officials of both nations to understand each other. I made members of the media aware of the event. But the logistics of the event were overwhelming for just one person.

I went to my colleagues and asked them to help me with preparations for the one-day event. To my delight, everyone I asked was willing to help me. Some helped compile press packets to hand out to members of the media. Others assisted with greeting the members of Congress as they came and left. Despite the many moving parts of the event, my colleagues helped me make sure nothing fell through the cracks.

> *An attitude that is willing to help others move forward will actually help you move forward.*

The Chicago Tribune gave the forum front-page news coverage and several other news outlets reported on the event as well. My boss was thrilled. That event taught me the value of teamwork, and how important it was to have other team players willing to help. I was grateful to have their help, but I did not understand why my colleagues were willing to help me. They certainly didn't have to; my boss never told them they had to participate. I found out later they were willing to help me because I had been a team player for them on previous occasions.

Being a team player is important at your workplace. That involves being willing to go out of your way to help others. It means being willing to put the interests of others ahead of your own. And that requires being engaged as part of the team, instead of being focused solely on your own concerns.

The Apostle Paul describes a picture of how you should function in your workplace. "Do nothing from selfish ambition or conceit, but in humility count others more significant than yourselves. Let each of you look not only to his own interests, but also to the interests of others" (Philippians 2:3-4). You may say that it is the responsibility of the leaders to put these actions on display for the rest of the team to follow—and you would be correct. But you are in charge of how you respond to that leadership. Rick Whitted explains this idea well in his book, *Outgrow Your Space at Work.*

> There are two factors that comprise the basic character of an occupational environment. The first factor is based on how the leader leads. The second factor is based on how well a team works together. While management has direct control over their leadership, they can only influence teamwork. At the end of the day, everyone must make a decision to work well with others individually and collectively.[1]

You are the one who will decide what your actions will look like at work. Will you be the one to help move the team forward? Or will you hold the team back because you are looking out for yourself? An attitude that is willing to help others move forward will actually help *you* move forward. But you cannot expect people to help you if you aren't willing to help them.

In this section, we will explore what Engaged looks like. In each chapter about Engaged, I will pose a Self-Leadership question which ties back to a comment made by a survey respondent in a preceding chapter. In these next three chapters, we will explore the following three topics.

1. Dedication
When you are on the job, you are there to work. Show up on time, work hard, and avoid distractions. Get your work done in a timely fashion.

2. Morale

Your boss needs you to work as a team player by being a loyal employee, putting aside your personal agenda, and demonstrating the kind of leadership you would want to see from a boss.

3. Ownership

Display an ownership mentality. Be self-motivated and manage your time well. Focus on being responsible, being curious, and taking your job seriously.

I hope you will see in these next chapters how helping others on your team with an Engaged mentality towards the team will serve to benefit you as well.

Reflection Questions

1. How dedicated are you to your work?

2. How much do you help to foster morale at your workplace?

3. How much do you have an ownership mentality toward the work you do?

Notes

[1] Rick Whitted, *Outgrow Your Space at Work: How to Thrive at Work and Build a Successful Career* (Grand Rapids: Revell, 2016), 130.

CHAPTER 20

Dedication

"The dedicated life is worth living."

—Annie Dillard

Building the ark was a daunting task for Noah. With only his three sons to help him (Genesis 6:10; 7:13), he built a boat that was approximately 450-500 feet long, 75-85 feet wide, and 45-50 feet tall.[1] Using the tools available at the time, this feat could have taken him 120 years (Genesis 6:3).

During those years, Noah no doubt dealt with ridicule from his neighbors. The people around him would have thought it absurd that water might cover the whole earth. People likely laughed at the man building the big boat. Noah must have persevered with extraordinary dedication through the mocking and laughing to accomplish his task.

Noah had to prepare his mind to appreciate the significance of his work in order to complete it. The mindset you bring to your work significantly affects what you will get out of it. Kenman Wong and Scott Rae summarize this idea well in their book *Business for the Common Good*.

Our job may not feel like we are doing God's will, but how it feels to us and what it actually is may be two very different things. ... Our work can well be our ministry [because ultimately we] all serve God full-time. ... The term *full-time ministry* should be used to refer to one's attitude toward service more than an arena of service. The term should describe an orientation toward serving God, rather than specific activities ... that are deemed to be serving God.[2]

Building a boat may not have seemed like a spiritual thing to do, but Noah's dedication to that work honored God. Your dedication to your work—or your dedication to serving God *through* your work—is a spiritual decision you must make every day. In Chapter Five, one of the bosses who responded to the survey said she wanted her employees to know that "if they show up and do their work we won't have issues." In response, the Self-Leadership Question for this chapter is: *Are you dedicated to your work?*

Pour your whole self into what you do. Remember that you are not just working for your boss; you are ultimately working for God.

You can choose to be dedicated to your work every day. Here are three things you can do each day to help you develop that dedication.

1. Show up

Make sure you are dedicated enough to your work to show up at the appropriate time. In fact, make sure that you are at your workplace early so that you can be *ready* when your day begins.

When you show up, make sure *all of you* shows up. Have the right mindset when you get to work, so you know that you are there to work. When you leave at the end of the day, make sure you know what you should focus on when you arrive the next day. That will help you start the next day with the right mindset as well.

2. Work hard

Show your dedication through what you do while you are at your job. When you are at work, make sure you work hard. That is what you are there for. That is what you get paid for. And that is what you want to be known for.

Your dedication to your work—or your dedication to serving God through your work—is a spiritual decision you must make every day.

Use your time wisely on the job. Pour your whole self into what you do. Remember that you are not just working for your boss; you are ultimately working for God (Ephesians 6:5-7; Colossians 3:22-23).

3. Avoid distractions

When you are on the job, make sure that you stay focused on what you are there to do. Do not allow yourself to be distracted. You are not paid to be distracted. Even if others want you to slack off, don't join in. You are there to work.

Keep your head in your work. Do not allow yourself to entertain resentment, accusations, or anger against your boss or your colleagues. That will not help you. That will only drag you down and prevent you from putting forth your best effort.

Your dedication has little to do with what kind of work you do, and much to do with the attitude you bring to it. Choose to be a light that burns brightly where you work, regardless of how dark you feel your workplace is. You could be the brightest light that any of your colleagues will ever see.

Reflection Questions

1. How often do you fully "show up" to work?

2. How hard do you work at your workplace?

3. How much do you get distracted at your workplace?

Notes

[1] http://worldwideflood.com/ark/noahs_cubit/cubit.htm, accessed June 1, 2018.

[2] Kenman L. Wong and Scott B. Rae, *Business for the Common Good: A Christian Vision for the Marketplace* (Madison, WI: InterVarsity Press, 2011), 56, 58.

CHAPTER 21

Morale

"The reality is that the only way change comes is when you lead by example."

—Anne Wojcicki

Many years ago, I worked at an organization that had horrible morale. To make matters worse, my boss was oblivious and even indifferent to the workplace culture. Despite his lack of interest in the culture, he was open to my starting a weekly prayer meeting at the office. I invited anyone and everyone on the staff to participate. I didn't expect many people to join me, but Joe and Tom did. Sometimes only two of us showed up for prayer, but more often than not the three of us were there.

Long after we started praying together, Tom surprised me one day. He said, "I know the only reason that I have been able to make it through is because of our prayers." He directly attributed that small prayer gathering to giving him the peace to survive the toxic work environment. Things at work didn't seem to change that much. But Tom, Joe, and I were changed. And that helped to change the morale of the workplace—at least from our perspective.

> *If you are willing to put the needs of the team ahead of yourself, people will ultimately look to you as a leader—because you are already leading.*

You might not be the one in charge. But you can make a difference—because you can choose to do something. If you are willing to put the needs of the team ahead of yourself, people will ultimately look to you as a leader—because you are already leading.

In his book *Give and Take*, Adam Grant explains that givers end up better off than takers. "Although we often stereotype givers as chumps and doormats, they turn out to be surprisingly successful[;] they get to the top without cutting others down, finding ways of expanding the pie that benefit themselves and the people around them."[1] Those who give of themselves to help others actually help themselves. As Scripture says, "give, and it will be given to you. Good measure, pressed down, shaken together, running over, will be put into your lap. For with the measure you use it will be measured back to you" (Luke 6:38).

Helping others will benefit the organization and it will benefit *you* in the process. In Chapter Five, one boss who participated in the survey said she wanted her employees to know that "we are all part of the team." Accordingly, the Self-Leadership Question for this chapter is: *Are you willing to help improve the morale at your workplace?*

Here are three ways that you can focus on working together as a team to improve morale.

1. Be concerned about others

By being a team player, you gain the notice and the respect of your boss and colleagues. If you go out of your way to help others, you will impact the people around you. In *Give and Take*, Adam Grant says that "putting the group's goals and mission first, and showing the same amount of concern for others as you do for yourself," is what makes everyone more successful—because there's more success "for the whole team to share."[2] When you make others successful, you will become more successful as well.

> *When you make others successful, you will become more successful as well.*

2. Be loyal

Put aside any differences you may have with management and work for the betterment of the organization. You are both parts of the same team, so focus on being loyal to the team.

You may feel that it's not worth being loyal to the company you work for. Then go out and find another job. But as long as you are there, put the organization ahead of your self-interest—because you will benefit in the process (Jeremiah 29:7).

Remember: this is not about the company you work for. This is about helping you enjoy your work more. You will get more by giving more.

3. Be the leader you wish your boss would be

You can set yourself up for leadership by learning from your boss—even if your boss is not a good leader. Determine what you think your boss does poorly—and do the opposite. If your boss is lazy, then be industrious. If your boss blames everyone else for his or her failures, then take responsibility for your mistakes. Resist the temptation to do what you see the boss is doing wrong.

Instead of complaining about the poor morale, I did something about it. Even though I wished my boss would have started the prayer meeting, I initiated the change I wanted to see.

By doing the right thing, you will set yourself up for being a good leader when the time comes—even if it's not at your current place of employment. By practicing now, you will prepare yourself for leadership when the opportunity presents itself.

You have more influence than you may realize. Only by making the effort to utilize that influence will you realize just how much you can improve the morale at your workplace.

Reflection Questions

1. How much are you concerned about others at your workplace?

2. How loyal are you to your employer?

3. To what degree are you the leader you wish your boss would be?

Notes
_____

[1] Adam Grant, *Give and Take: Why Helping Others Drives Our Success* (New York: Penguin Books, 2013), 9, 258.

[2] Ibid, 74-75.

CHAPTER 22

Ownership

"In a very real way, ownership is the very essence of leadership."

—Henry Cloud

Several years ago, I oversaw some annual events for the organization I worked for. Sometimes several dozen people would attend, sometimes a smaller number. But regardless of the number of attendees, there were innumerable details that had to be coordinated. And to handle all those details, I turned to Beth.

I knew as soon as I handed the event off to Beth, it was as good as done. She came back to me only if she had questions. She handled every single detail with perfect ease. She could run an intimate event, a small conference, or even a large convention. That's because she took ownership of whatever she was asked to do.

I remember the many phone conversations with Beth. I would ask her, "What do we need to do about *this*?" And she would inevitably say, "Already taken care of." While still on the call, I would think of something else and ask, "Have you been able to deal with *that*?" And again, she would say, "I've already got it covered."

> *God has given you talents. It's your responsibility to use them to the best of your ability.*

Beth led by taking ownership of her role. She understood what was expected of her, and she expanded her role by thinking through everything that was involved with her responsibilities. As a result, her job was done well, and the organization benefitted as well.

You can take ownership of your responsibilities by doing what Rick Whitted says in *Outgrow Your Space at Work*. "If you already know everything about your current job, figure out how to do it better, quicker, or cheaper. Help others around you get better, and act like you're glad to be a part of the organization."[1] By being willing to pitch in and do what is necessary, you will become invaluable to everyone around you.

You do not have to wait for someone else's permission to take ownership of your situation. Your boss wants you to take charge of your job. In Chapter Five, one boss respondent said she wished her employees knew "how to be responsible, how to be curious, how to take their job seriously." Similarly, this chapter's Self-Leadership Question is: *Do you take ownership of your work?*

Based on this boss's response to the survey, these are three actions to focus on in your workplace.

1. Be responsible

The Apostle Paul made it clear that you must focus on being responsible for the work that you do. "Make a careful exploration of who you are and the work you have been given, and then sink yourself into that. Don't be impressed with yourself. Don't compare yourself with others. Each of you must take responsibility for doing the creative best you can with your own life" (Galatians 6:4-5 MSG).

If you have to depend on someone else to make you do your job, then you are not being responsible. Make the decision that you will be fully present at your job and take responsibility for yourself. Do not look to anyone else to tell you what to do. God has given you talents. It's your responsibility to use them to the best of your ability (Matthew 25:21, 23).

2. Be curious

Curiosity requires that you have your eyes wide open. You have to be observant to notice what's going on around you. Therefore, be *intentionally* curious. You will notice only what you look for.

> *You will notice only what you look for.*

Be willing to ask questions. Figure out how you can do your job better. Learn how your colleagues are getting results. Become a constant learner within your field.

Once you have learned how to do your job better, ask how you can be helpful beyond what you are currently doing. Find out how other divisions do what they are doing. See how the work you are doing can be completed in a way that expedites or improves the entire process for the company. Use your intentional curiosity to make yourself invaluable.

3. Take your job seriously

Work is work. There's no other way around it. Nonetheless, dive in and give it your all. As the Scripture says, "don't just do the minimum that will get you by. Do your best. Work from the heart" (Colossians 3:23 MSG).

Beth did her work well because she knew that others were counting on her. She made her work a priority. She invested herself in becoming an expert in her field, and she became an invaluable resource to me and the rest of our colleagues.

The same intensity that you bring to caring for your family and hobbies should be reflected at your workplace. Everyone there should see that when you are at work, you are there to contribute to making the organization the best it can be.

Take ownership of your role at work like Beth did. Go out of your way to take responsibility for yourself and the work that you do. Be a serious contributor to the success of everyone around you. And you will likewise reap the benefit of your efforts.

Reflection Questions

1. How much have you taken responsibility for yourself at work?

2. How curious have you been at work up to this point?

3. How seriously have you taken your job?

Notes

[1] Rick Whitted, *Outgrow Your Space at Work: How to Thrive at Work and Build a Successful Career* (Grand Rapids: Revell, 2016), 178-179.

PART III
MAKING THE CHANGE

In Part Three, we will explore the means through which you can make significant change in your life by exercising your Self-Leadership. In the following chapters, we will identify how you can implement the changes outlined in the Self-Leadership paradigm.

Chapter 25:   **Implementation Step #2 – What You Say**
Deliberately focus on the words that you say. By taking responsibility for what you say about yourself and those around you, you will be in a better position to improve your relationships.

Chapter 26:   **Implementation Step #3 – What You Do**
Deliberately focus on what you do. By taking responsibility for what you do—and making it a natural outgrowth of what you think and say—you will be in a better position to achieve what you want in your career and life.

Chapter 27:   **Implementation Step #4 – What You Permit**
Be serious about follow through. If you allow behavior that goes against what you think, say, and do, you will undermine all of your active efforts to change yourself.

Why It Matters

By implementing these intentional steps, you can change how you perceive yourself. And you can use your newfound understanding to effect the change you want to see in yourself and in your work environment.

CHAPTER 23

Implementing the New Paradigm

"If you want small changes in your life, work on your attitude.
But if you want big and primary changes,
work on your paradigm."

—Stephen R. Covey

People view the world through a paradigm. It's how we make sense of the world. But there are times that our paradigm is not helping us, and we may realize we need to make a change in how we think. As I mentioned in the Introduction, I was very selfish and self-centered when I was in college. I believed the world revolved around me, but that belief left me feeling empty and lonely. Through reading the Bible, I saw that Jesus' teachings were the opposite of my way of doing things; I also saw how those teachings provided the peace that I didn't have. I starting exploring a way of thinking that was contrary to my current belief system. And I was willing to make a paradigm shift.

Be aware of your paradigm. By questioning the way you look at things, you will improve the quality of your perspective. As Alan Jacobs explains in *How to Think*, "if you learn to think, genuinely to *think*, you *will* sometimes change your mind."[1] Dr. Jacobs then offers this encouragement to become open to changing how you think: "What is needed for the life of thinking is *hope*: hope of knowing more, understanding more, *being* more than we currently are."[2]

Changing your thinking to fit with the Self-Leadership paradigm will take time. The change will not come overnight. Nonetheless, with intentional design and consistent implementation, you will begin to see changes in yourself.

Over the past seventeen chapters, we have explored in depth what HOPE looks like. To review the main components of HOPE, below are the four topics discussed in Part Two.

Honoring
Respect the position that your boss holds, even if you do not think your boss deserves that honor. You should also express your appreciation and support for what your boss does for you.

Open
Have open communication with your boss. This means not only being honest with your boss, but also freely sharing information in a timely manner.

Perceptive
Try to see the big picture in the organization. Look beyond yourself and see how what you do affects everyone else—especially when it comes to interfacing with customers.

Engaged
Recognize that employees and management are two parts of the same team. As an employee, you must work hard on the job and be self-motivated. You must hold yourself to the same standard you hold your boss to.

The Self-Leadership paradigm will change how you view yourself. With this new lens, you will be able to redefine how you view everything else at your workplace.

As we move into Part Three, we will further explore how to apply these concepts. In the following chapters, you will find a guide to help you change how you look at yourself and your workplace using a strategy composed of these four actions.

> *The Self-Leadership paradigm will change how you view yourself. With this new lens, you will be able to redefine how you view everything else at your workplace.*

What You Think

Deliberately focus on the thoughts in your head. By screening what you think about yourself and those around you, you will be in a better position to take control of your outlook.

What You Say

Deliberately focus on the words that you say. By taking responsibility for what you say about yourself and those around you, you will be in a better position to improve your relationships.

What You Do

Deliberately focus on what you do. By taking responsibility for what you do—and making it a natural outgrowth of what you think and say—you will be in a better position to achieve what you want in your career and life.

What You Permit

Be serious about follow through. If you allow behavior that goes against what you think, say, and do, you will undermine all of your active efforts to change yourself.

Over the next four chapters, we will discuss how focusing on these four actions will help you effect the change you want to see in yourself and your workplace. As I mentioned before, personal change will require intentionality of design and consistency of implementation over a prolonged period of time.

Change is hard. Changing yourself is even harder. It is my hope and prayer that you will be able to see how you can benefit through the change—and how others around you can benefit as well.

Reflection Questions

1. Which tenet of HOPE—Honoring, Open, Perceptive, or Engaged—do you find most appealing?

2. Which tenet of HOPE do you need to work on the most?

3. What first step can you take to upgrade your Self-Leadership?

Notes
_____

[1] Alan Jacobs, *How to Think: A Survival Guide for a World at Odds* (New York: Currency, 2017), 149.

[2] Ibid, 151.

CHAPTER 24

Implementation Step #1
What You Think

*"If you realized how powerful your thoughts are,
you would never think a negative thought."*

—Peace Pilgrim

Twenty years ago I went through a dark time. I was in between jobs for a year. I did everything I knew to do: talk to my network, connect with acquaintances, conduct informational interviews, reach out to new contacts, attend job fairs, answer job advertisements, write thank you notes, and follow up. But nothing resulted from all my efforts. It was taking its toll on me financially—and emotionally.

If I have ever been depressed, it was at that time. I heard the voices of self-doubt, defeatism, and hopelessness reverberating in my mind all the time. My thinking had gone into a downward spiral. I was beginning to despair of ever being employed again.

One day, I said I had had enough. I pulled out ... my Bible. And I began to search the Scriptures to remind me who I was. I had to stop listening to what everything around me told me I was. And I had to listen to what God said about my worth. I had to remind myself what was true because I can't believe everything I think.

At that time I was reading my Bible every morning. I was spending time with God every day. But that wasn't enough to combat the voices that were telling me I was worthless. I found I had to go even deeper. I had to fight the lies with the truth.

There will be times that you will have similar situations. You will feel beat down by circumstances—and sometimes you won't know why. You will get stuck in a negative thought pattern, and you won't know how to get out of it. You will be tempted to doubt yourself, and you won't know what to do about it. When these situations come upon you, you must realize that you can't believe everything *you* think. But you can *control* what you think.

As the Apostle Paul said to the Church at Philippi, "whatever is true, whatever is honorable, whatever is just, whatever is

> *Your thinking can go astray more easily than you may realize—especially if you don't realize your thinking can go astray.*

pure, whatever is lovely, whatever is commendable, if there is any excellence, if there is anything worthy of praise, think about these things" (Philippians 4:8). It is important to fill your mind with what is true. Be careful about what thoughts you allow into your mind. You have to be mindful of what your mind's full of—because you can't believe everything you think.

Jesus asked his disciples and the crowds he taught, "What do you think?" (Matthew 17:25; 18:12; 21:28). Clearly Jesus wanted you to think. But he also wanted you to be aware of *what* you think (2 Corinthians 10:5).

In his letter to the Romans, Paul told them to exercise their minds: "Do not be conformed to this world, but be transformed by the renewal of your mind" (Romans 12:2a). Do not think how everybody else thinks. Think for yourself.

Be aware of what you are thinking at your workplace. Be conscious of the thoughts you entertain. You can't believe everything you think. Rick Whitted in *Outgrow Your Space at Work* explains how you can dupe yourself into believing something that isn't true.

> *Seeing who you can be leads to believing you can be that person which leads to being that person.*

> Accenture, a management consulting firm, conducted a survey in which people were asked the reasons for their lack of career progression. Almost two-thirds blamed the company. Two-fifths were convinced that their current organization provided no real opportunity for advancement or no clear career path. Another one-fifth indicated that it was their boss or supervisor's fault for the perceived lack of career advancement. *The overwhelming majority didn't consider one behavior or attitude they could've personally changed to improve their opportunity to advance. ...*

> [You are] inclined to interpret what happens in the workplace based on a biased view of yourself. You think you're being objective—even when you're not.[1]

Your thinking can go astray more easily than you may realize—especially if you don't realize your thinking *can* go astray. You can't believe everything you think. In becoming aware of how you think, here are some guidelines to help you exert your Self-Leadership and become the person you want to be.

1. Believe who you can be

In order to become the person you want to be, you must first have a vision of who you want to become. *Seeing* who you can be leads to *believing* you can be that person which leads to *being* that person.

You can get a vision of who you can become by understanding how God sees you. Fill your mind with what the Scripture says about you—just like I had to do. Then believe you are who God says you are.

The Scripture says that you are

- God's workmanship, created to do good works (Ephesians 2:10),
- The salt of the earth and the light of the world (Matthew 5:13-14), and
- A minister of reconciliation (2 Corinthians 5:17-21).

If you have been told by others that's not who you are, then you will have to relearn who you are—by reminding yourself of what the Scripture says.

2. Believe it's not about you

Your life is not about you. You are here for the benefit of others, not for yourself. Therefore, you owe it to those around you to constantly be learning how to be better.

If you are filled with yourself, then there is no room for anyone else in your life. Instead, you must always be thinking of others. Remember: humility is not thinking less of yourself. It's about thinking of yourself less.

3. Believe the best of others

In Matthew 18:21, Peter asked Jesus how many times he had to forgive when his brother sinned against him. Peter thought that seven times would be more than enough. In verse 22, Jesus answered Peter's question: he had to forgive his brother seventy-seven times. Jesus wasn't saying we should keep score of how many times someone has wronged us. He was saying we should be prepared to forgive people often.

I've often noticed that wherever there is *contact* between people, there is *conflict* between people. But even when that happens at your workplace, you can choose to forgive those people. You are supposed to wipe the slate clean every time you forgive someone. Even if you don't *feel* like forgiving, you have to decide that you *will* forgive. By making the decision to forgive, your emotions will follow.

It's important to note that the people you work with don't have to ask for forgiveness before you can forgive them. Remember: Jesus asked the Father to forgive those who crucified him—even though they didn't repent—because they didn't know what they were doing (Luke 23:34a). You can do the same thing. You can choose to forgive, even if they aren't sorry, because they likely don't know what they are doing. That's the forgiveness Jesus is talking about.

> *If you are filled with yourself, then there is no room for anyone else in your life.*

Your thoughts have profound consequences. Know what you think. Course correct what you think when your thoughts go awry. But don't believe everything you think.

Reflection Questions

1. Who do you believe you are?

2. How self-focused is your thinking?

3. How easily are you able to forgive others?

Notes
_____

[1] Rick Whitted, *Outgrow Your Space at Work: How to Thrive at Work and Build a Successful Career* (Grand Rapids: Revell, 2016), 184, 187. Emphasis added.

CHAPTER 25

Implementation Step #2
What You Say

"You are not only responsible for what you say,
but also for what you do not say."

—Martin Luther

A long time ago I worked for a boss who was extremely direct. He had developed quite a reputation from the things he would say. Those who agreed with him loved his forthright style. But those who disagreed with him did not appreciate his frank comments. He did what he thought was right, and he did not equivocate from that stance. No one could sway him from what he believed. He did not fear anyone and spoke his mind freely. But he seemed to be unaware of the collateral damage from his statements.

He did not compromise on anything, and he did not back down from what he said, and that combination had the potential to turn people off. Over time his influence waned because he alienated the very people who agreed with him in the first place.

The Scripture makes it clear that words have a powerful effect on people (James 3:5-10). I know everybody puts their foot in their mouth. I've gotten rather accustomed to the taste of mine. But even the offhand words you say have tremendous impact. My boss discovered that the hard way.

> *You don't need prior authorization to say something nice.*

I am convinced that words can do much damage—especially emotional and spiritual damage. When I was a kid, I heard the schoolyard chant, "Sticks and stones may break my bones, but words will never hurt me." Sadly, that phrase is just not true. Proverbs 18:14 says that your spirit will sustain your infirmity. But what do you do when you have a wounded spirit? A broken bone can heal, but many people never heal from the wounds made by words.

At the same time, words can do great good. Proverbs 16:24 says that pleasant words are like honeycomb, sweet to the soul, and health to the bones. You can build up others with your words. Think through the opportunity you have to exert your Self-Leadership in what you say. To help you capitalize on that opportunity, here are three ways for evaluating and choosing the words to say.

1. Say what you mean, and mean what you say
When you talk to others, be direct. Make sure that you say what you mean and mean what you say. If you don't mean it, don't say it.

People joke about what they don't want to be serious about. And people put down others as a way of complimenting them. But when people do that, they are not communicating directly. Then there is confusion about what they meant. And that causes relational damage (Proverbs 26:18-19).

If you mean "yes," then say "yes." If you mean "no," then say "no." Saying anything other than that causes more problems than you want to have to deal with (Matthew 5:37).

2. Say words that build up, not tear down

Consider what you say before you say it. You *can* and *should* control your tongue (James 1:26), as my boss should have done.

Often when people say what they really think—like my boss did—they do it without trying to control their tongue. But it doesn't have to be that way. In a blog interview at RobertMcFarland.net, entrepreneur Nathan Tabor explains

> how you deal with your personal life—your walk with God—really affects tremendously how your business life will be. ... The proverb principle "a soft answer turns away wrath"—take that and apply it to your business world when you're getting ready to argue with a partner, or you have a deal that's going south, or someone is yelling at you about something. Instead of yelling back, take the approach of ... "I'm really sorry that that's happened so let's see what we can do to work that out." It's amazing how that will calm that situation.[1]

Remember that death and life are in the power of the tongue (Proverbs 18:21). You may be the only one who understands the importance of this truth at your workplace. Even if your boss doesn't understand the power of the tongue, you can be the source of life-affirming words that will build up everyone you come in contact with. Don't miss the opportunity to speak words of life: "Do not repay evil for evil or reviling for

Say the words to others that you would want others to say to you.

reviling, but on the contrary, bless, for to this you were called, that you may obtain a blessing" (1 Peter 3:9).

3. Say what you want to say, and don't hide it

You have an opportunity to make a difference in people's lives. Don't squander the opportunity. You don't need prior authorization to say something nice. And you don't have to be dubbed Chief Morale Officer before you speak words of life.

Say the words to others that you would want others to say to you (Matthew 7:12). Before long, the words that you say will eventually be said to you (Ecclesiastes 11:1).

The words you say have great power. You may never even know the full impact your words will have on the people around you.

Allow what you think to have an effect on what you say. The more you can control what you think, the more you can speak transformational words to those around you.

Reflection Questions

1. How often do you mean what you say? How often do you say what you mean?

2. How often do you say words that build up? How often do you say words that tear down?

3. How often do you say what you really want to say?

Notes

[1] "Practical Spiritual Disciplines to Improve Your Business Success," http://www. robertmcfarland.net/practical-spiritual-disciplines-to-improve-your-business-success/, accessed November 21, 2018.

CHAPTER 26

Implementation Step #3
What You Do

"What you are will show in what you do."
—Thomas Edison

More than twenty years ago I volunteered in a statewide campaign for attorney general. I lived in Northern Virginia at the time, so I threw myself into helping at the local office in Fairfax. At one point I had the opportunity to meet Kevin, the deputy campaign manager. Kevin was in the Richmond headquarters office, so we didn't have much contact at the time. After the campaign, I saw him at statewide events for several years, but then we didn't have any contact for more than a decade.

Then out of the blue, Kevin contacted me when he saw I was speaking at a national conference he was attending. He asked to get together, and as a result we started a friendship that was barely an acquaintance a dozen years before. That meeting opened the door for several lucrative opportunities for my consultancy.

> **Serve others in your job the way that you would want others to serve you in their jobs.**

I had no idea that meeting Kevin would become valuable to me two decades later. There is no way I could have known that volunteering on that campaign would prompt Kevin to reach out to me. But I did know that working hard as a volunteer would reflect well on me later on.

You can't determine ahead of time which professional relationships will be the ones that will benefit you the most. You never know who can help you down the road, so be conscientious to do your work in a way that will reflect well on you. Here's how you should work so that you—and God—will be pleased with the result.

1. Do your best work

The most spiritual thing you can do in your current job is to do it with excellence. King Solomon said you should work hard at whatever you do (Ecclesiastes 9:10). Jesus said you should give more than is expected of you (Matthew 5:40-41). And the Apostle Paul said you should do your work as if you were doing it for God and not for your boss (Ephesians 6:5-7; Colossians 3:23-24).

Tim Keller, former senior pastor of Redeemer Presbyterian Church, extends this thought further in his book *Every Good Endeavor*. "One of the main ways that you love others in your work is through the 'ministry of competence.' If God's purpose for your job is that you serve the human community, then the way to serve God best is to do the job as well as it can be done."[1]

Your job is not just about showing up at work every day. It's about using your time and your abilities to showcase your love for God and your concern for others. And you show that love and concern the most when you do your best work.

2. Do what you would want others to do

Serve others in your job the way that you would want others to serve you in their jobs. You can't do work that is not your best and then be surprised when others do it to you. As Jesus said, do to others whatever you want them to do to you (Matthew 7:12).

No one would be pleased to hire someone to do a job for them— whether it is brain surgery or lawn maintenance—and find it's been done carelessly or negligently. And yet people think it's acceptable to give half-hearted effort at their own job. No one should expect to do just the minimum and believe they will be applauded for it.

As Tim Keller says, you serve God and the human community in your job through your "ministry of competence." If you don't do your best, then the human community misses out and God is not honored.

Let the person that you are— and the person that you want to become—be reflected in the work that you do each and every day.

3. Do your work how you want to be remembered

You never know who you might end up working with someday. Even if you leave your current job, you may see those colleagues again in your career. How you work now will affect how they will remember you in the future.

How will the Kevins in your life view you? Will they recommend you to others, or will they want nothing to do with you? You have no idea how many Kevins are watching you now. What you think no one else sees will likely become known (Luke 12:3).

Be the person you want to be known as. You do not have to stay the way you are now. You can become who want to be. But that means you have to be that person every day—starting right now.

The quality of your work will reflect on you more than you might realize. Do your current job the best that you can. Let the person that you are—and the person that you want to become—be reflected in the work that you do each and every day.

Reflection Questions

1. How often do you do your best work?

2. How often do you settle for less than your best work?

3. What level of effort do you want to be known for doing?

Notes

1 Timothy Keller, *Every Good Endeavor: Connecting Your Work to God's Work* (New York: Riverhead, 2014), 67.

CHAPTER 27

Implementation Step #4
What You Permit

We should never permit ourselves to do anything
that we are not willing to see our children do.

—Brigham Young

When God told Joshua to lead the Israelites to displace the peoples in the land of Canaan, they obediently followed Joshua's leadership and took possession of the land. Then Joshua divided the land with God's guidance and gave each tribe their inheritance, even though some of the Canaanites still lived in the land (Joshua 13:1-7). Before Joshua died, he reminded the Israelites that they had to stand strong.

> Then Joshua said to the people, "You are witnesses against yourselves that you have chosen the LORD, to serve him." And they said, "We are witnesses." He said, "Then put away the foreign gods that are among you, and incline your heart to the LORD, the God of Israel." And the people said to Joshua, "The LORD our God we will serve, and his voice we will obey." (Joshua 24:22-24)

The Israelites thought the right thoughts, said the right words, and did the right things. They had seen the LORD do amazing things through them. And they said they would do all that they should do from this point forward. But then something happened.

> When Joshua dismissed the people, the people of Israel went each to his inheritance to take possession of the land. And the people served the LORD all the days of Joshua, and all the days of the elders who outlived Joshua, who had seen all the great work that the LORD had done for Israel. … And there arose another generation after them who did not know the LORD or the work that he had done for Israel. And the people of Israel did what was evil in the sight of the LORD and served the Baals. And they abandoned the LORD, the God of their fathers, who had brought them out of the land of Egypt. They went after other gods, from among the gods of the peoples who were around them, and bowed down to them. And they provoked the LORD to anger. (Judges 2:6-7, 10b-12)

The Israelites did the valiant deeds God required, but they didn't do the small actions that God expected. They could do the difficult things when times were hard, but not the simple things when times were easy. They didn't teach their children what God had done for them. They didn't explain God's mandate to their children. Instead, they permitted the next generation to drift.

If you are not progressing, you are regressing.

If you allow your situation to continue the way it is and assume that you are holding your ground, then you are mistaken. If you are not gaining ground, you are losing ground. Just like money not invested will lose value due to inflation, you cannot maintain the status quo. If you are not *progressing*, you are *regressing*.

You may know the right things to think, say, and do, but what you permit to stay in your life can negate all of that. Being intentional is not sufficient; you must also be consistent. Habits will creep subtly into your life, so you must be on your guard.

To help you be aware, here are three things to watch for.

> *You may have all the right actions, words, and even thoughts. But if you allow other things in your life to take root, they will choke your zeal for what you think, say, and do.*

1. Changes in priorities

Be careful if you notice a change in priorities. The problem is that you likely won't notice the change in priorities in yourself. The Israelites did not see those changes in themselves, and neither did they hold each other accountable for those changes. Enlist friends, family, or a coach to tell you if they see any undesirable changes in you. People who know you well can spot those changes, so ask them to help you stay on track.

2. Rationalizations

Before you notice changes in your priorities, you may find yourself making compromises in your standards. It's easy to make rationalizations. But watch out. It's a small thing that can snowball.

It's helpful to have someone who can call you out on those rationalizations. But be conscious of how you respond. If you react defensively, that's a sure sign that they are right.

When you make a rationalization, you are like the frog in the pot. If you put a frog in a pot and slowly turn up the heat, it won't notice that the water is getting warmer—until it's cooked. Every rationalization turns the heat up on the pot. Avoid making rationalizations, so you won't get into the pot in the first place.

3. Waning enthusiasm

Before you notice yourself making rationalizations, you may find your enthusiasm waning. Others may notice a change in what you were once passionate about, and you will need them to speak into your life if they see it happen. Again, this change can be slow and subtle, but it is something to be mindful of nonetheless. You may have all the right actions, words, and even thoughts. But if you allow other things in your life to take root, they will choke your zeal for what you think, say, and do.

Be watchful for what you permit in your life. Be vigilant, and allow others in your life to help you stay focused.

Reflection Questions

1. When have you or others noticed your enthusiasm wane for something you said was important? What did you do about it?

2. When have you or others noticed compromises in your standards? What did you do about it?

3. When have you or others noticed changes in your priorities? What did you do about it?

CHAPTER 28

Conclusion

"True strength lies in submission which permits one to dedicate his life, through devotion, to something beyond himself."

—Henry Miller

When the Roman soldiers came to apprehend Jesus in the garden of Gethsemane, Jesus made sure they were aware of how and why this situation came to pass.

> Don't you realize that I am able right now to call to my Father, and twelve companies—more, if I want them—of fighting angels would be here, battle-ready? But if I did that, how would the Scriptures come true that say this is the way it has to be?" Then Jesus addressed the mob: "What is this— coming out after me with swords and clubs as if I were a dangerous criminal? Day after day I have been sitting in the Temple teaching, and you never so much as lifted a hand against me. You've done it this way to confirm and fulfill the prophetic writings." (Matthew 26:53-56a MSG)

Even though Jesus had the ability to request all the power of heaven to save him, he relinquished it in the Garden of Gethsemane.

He wanted the soldiers—and his disciples—to know that he voluntarily submitted his will to his Father's will. As Jesus prayed earlier that night in Gethsemane, "My Father, if it be possible, let this cup pass from me; nevertheless, not as I will, but as you will" (Matthew 26:39).

That submission of his will to the Father's demonstrated a supreme act of Self-Leadership. As I have already said, Self-Leadership is an important practice to cultivate. And submission is an important part of developing that Self-Leadership.

> *In order to become a good leader, you must first become a good follower.*

Submission is a spiritual principle that has powerful application in the natural realm (1 Corinthians 10:33-11:1). You must be willing to submit to a higher authority to prepare yourself for leading others. In order to become a good leader, you must first become a good follower.

Submission means putting aside your own desires for the benefit of others. That's why it is so hard. And that's why it is so important—not only in the workplace, but also at home. God designed the social order based on submission to authority, as Jesus evidenced in the Garden of Gethsemane. The principle of submission in Self-Leadership applies to everyone.

Using your Self-Leadership, here are three ways in which you can improve your ability to lead.

1. Lead yourself first
Be content where you are now. Focus on doing your best work in your current job. That will prepare you for larger responsibilities.

Do not get caught up with titles or position (Psalm 131:1). Others will recognize you as a leader when you lead yourself. The larger positions will come if you are found faithful in what you do now (Luke 19:17).

2. Lead by example

Be willing to lead by example. Jesus submitted to the Father so that the Scriptures could be fulfilled, and so that we could have an example to follow. As Jesus said in John's gospel, "I seek not my own will but the will of him who sent me" (John 5:30b).

As I said earlier, you must be intentional and consistent in your example. Honor your boss, even behind his or her back. You must give respect in order to earn it.

Be a leader so others can have an example to emulate. They need to see what Self-Leadership looks like in action. They will not do what you say; they will do what you do.

3. Lead through submission.

Demonstrate Self-Leadership by willingly submitting to your boss. You must be willing to submit to those in authority over you in order to be a leader. Why should anyone put you in leadership if you will not submit to others' leadership? You cannot expect others to follow you if you do not follow your boss's lead.

> *You can lead through submitting to your boss.*

God designed submission to authority to benefit you (Ephesians 5:21-23). Submitting is not about being a doormat for someone else. It's about reflecting Jesus in your actions.

If you try to circumvent God's design of submission to authority, it will not go well with you. But if you submit to your boss, you demonstrate your leadership through your followership—just like

Christ did when he submitted to his Father, saying "not my will, but yours be done" (Luke 22:42b).

Be the employee you would want to work for you. That will help your boss become the boss you would want to report to. You do not have to wait for your boss to become the boss you want. You can lead through submitting to your boss.

Reflection Questions

1. In what ways have you led by following? How can you lead at work by following your boss now?

2. How do you need to change yourself to be the example you want to set for others?

3. How could (or should) you be a better follower?

CHAPTER 29

Epilogue

"You must be the change that you wish to see in the world."
—Mahatma Gandhi

As you start the process of Self-Leadership, think through how you want to end up. Figure out the impact you want to have, so you can become the person you want to be. Former Senate Chaplain Richard Halverson put this idea into perspective.

> You're going to meet an old man someday! Down the road—10, 20, 30 years—he'll be waiting there for you. You'll be catching up with him.
>
> What kind of an old man are you going to meet? He may be a seasoned, soft, gracious fellow—a gentleman that has grown old gracefully, surrounded by hosts of friends. Or he may be a bitter, disillusioned, dried-up, cynical old buzzard without a good word for anybody—soured, friendless and alone.
>
> That old man will be you. He'll be the composite of everything you do, say, think—today and tomorrow. His mind will be set in a mold you have made by your attitudes. His heart will be turning out what you've been putting in. Every little thought, every deed, goes into this old man.

Every day in every way you are becoming more and more like yourself. Amazing but true! You're getting to look more like yourself, think more like yourself, and talk more like yourself. You're becoming yourself more and more.

Live only in terms of what you're getting out of life, and the old man gets smaller, drier, harder, crabbier and more self-centered. Open your life to others, think in terms of what you can give, and the old man grows larger, softer, kindlier, and greater.[1]

The person that you are today is a compilation of the decisions that you have made up to this point. But you can change the person you will become by the decisions you make now.

As you think through what you want to do differently, it's important to think about how you will change *you*. You can't change your circumstances until you change yourself first.

> *You can't change your circumstances until you change yourself first.*

In fact, you will be the same person that you are right now in ten, twenty, or thirty years—unless you change these three things.

1. The books you read

To change *you*, first adjust your thinking. The most effective way to positively adjust your thinking is by being exposed to good ideas. And the best way to introduce yourself to good ideas is by reading good books.

By reading good books, you will refocus your thinking. In this hyper-marketed culture, you are constantly being assaulted by ideas. Only by reading good books can you fill your mind with the right thoughts.

I have many good business books, leadership books, and spiritual books in my library. If you'd like a starter reading list, contact me at www.WhatYourBossWishesYouKnew.com. (I will give you a hint as to what tops my reading list: it is the #1 best-selling book of all time.)

2. The people you meet
To change *you*, allow yourself to meet new people. You will become like the people you surround yourself with.

Think through what kind of person you want to become. What kind of people do you hang around now? How is the person you want to become different from them? What kind of people do you need to meet in order to become the person you want to be?

> *It's the little changes you make every day that will change you.*

The best way to meet the right people is to be where they are. Where do these people congregate? Where do you have to go to meet them? Find them, spend time with them, and get to know them. Eventually you will become like them.

3. The goals you set
To change the person you will become, set new goals for yourself. When you set goals, set *big* goals. As Johann Wolfgang von Goethe said, "Dream no small dreams, for they have no power to move the hearts of men."

To reach your goals, put good habits in place first. Your habits will be the tools you use to reach your goals. As Ralph Waldo Emerson famously said,

> *Sow a thought and you reap an action;*
> *sow an act and you reap a habit;*
> *sow a habit and you reap a character;*
> *sow a character and you reap a destiny.*[2]

It's the little changes you make every day that will change you. And it all starts with reading the right books, meeting the right people, and setting the right goals. (If you need help in setting the right goals, you can contact me at www.WhatYourBossWishesYouKnew.com. I'll be glad to point you in the right direction.)

Through intentionality and consistency, you can become the person you want to be. Through your Self-Leadership, you can become a person of HOPE—Honoring, Open, Perceptive, and Engaged. Through your Self-Leadership, you can control what you think, what you say, what you do, and what you permit. And through your Self-Leadership, you can put into practice what your boss wishes you knew.

Reflection Questions

1. What books do you read now? What books do you think you should be reading?

2. What kind of people do you hang around now? Who do you think you should hang around?

3. What goals do you have for yourself now? What goals do you want to achieve from now on?

Notes

[1] Daryl E. Witmer, "As time goes on, you become your choices," *Bangor Daily News*, February 3, 2007, accessed at https://archive.bangordailynews.com/2007/02/03/as-time-goes-on-you-become-your-choices/.

[2] https://www.goodreads.com/quotes/416934-sow-a-thought-and-you-reap-an-action-sow-an, accessed November 21, 2018.

Additional Research Questions and Findings

Below are the additional questions and the aggregated responses from the survey conducted by WPA Opinion Research (referenced in Chapter One).

Including yourself, what is the total number of people currently living in your household?

One	20%
Two	34%
Three or more	46%

Are there children in your household under the age of eighteen?

Yes	35%
No	65%

What was the last grade in school you completed?

High school graduate or less	32%
Some college	31%
College graduate or higher	37%

Was your TOTAL household income BEFORE taxes for 2015:

Less than $35,000	28%
$35,000 to less than $50,000	12%
$50,000 to less than $75,000	19%
$75,000 to less than $100,000	17%
$100,000 or more	24%

Which of the following describes your race?

White	61%
Hispanic, Mexican, Latino, Spanish	18%
African-American	12%
Other	9%

What is your age?

18-34	34%
35-44	22%
45-54	22%
55-64	16%
65 or over	6%

What is your gender?

Male	54%
Female	46%

Region:

Northeast	20%
Midwest	23%
South	35%
West	22%

Self-Leadership Diagnostic Tool

You can use these 12 questions as a self-diagnostic tool. On a scale of 0-5 with 0 being *not at all* and 5 being *the best possible,* rate your Self-Leadership.

Answer these questions as honestly as you can. You can find additional resources at www.WhatYourBossWishesYouKnew.com.

Honoring

_____ 1. Do you appreciate your boss?

_____ 2. Do you respect your boss?

_____ 3. Do you support your boss?

Open

_____ 1. Can you say what needs to be said in a straightforward but caring way?

_____ 2. Can you be counted on to exhibit integrity all the time?

_____ 3. Are you transparent with your boss?

Perceptive

_____ 1. Are you willing to see yourself from your boss's perspective?

_____ 2. Are you aware of the policies and procedures you should follow at your workplace?

_____ 3. Do you represent your employer well on and off the job?

Engaged

_____ 1. Are you dedicated to your work?

_____ 2. Are you willing to help improve the morale at your workplace?

_____ 3. Do you take ownership of your work?

About the Author

Robert McFarland is a leadership consultant, executive coach, and conference speaker. Robert has worked with myriad organizations conducting strategic planning, providing branding guidance, and giving communications counsel.

Robert is President of Transformational Impact LLC, a leadership development consultancy helping companies envision their preferred future, map the strategy to get there, and create the company culture to bring it to fruition. After serving evangelical ministries and nonprofits for 20 years as an executive, board member, and consultant, Robert founded Transformational Impact LLC to help for-profit companies and nonprofits capitalize on the power of their vision.

Robert enjoys helping people change their thinking, so they can get the results they want at work and in life. His Impactful Lives blog at www.RobertMcFarland.net focuses on how intentional Christians can lead their thinking in their spiritual lives and in their professional lives to lead impactful lives.

Robert serves as the Intentional Leadership Coach for the Intentional Living Center and is a frequent contributor to the Intentional Living broadcast and features. He is a member of the Board of Directors of the National Religious Broadcasters and the Chairman of the Board of Directors of The Family Foundation of Virginia.

Robert and his wife, Tamitha, recently moved their six children out of the Washington, D.C. area to the Shenandoah Valley of Virginia, where they now wake up to the sound of cows instead of cars.

Made in the
USA
Columbia, SC